THE BRIDGE BETWEEN THE EAST AND WEST:

A JOURNEY TO TRUTH THROUGH HIS LOVE

Teresita,

Con todo el amor
de Jesús y María
from your mom Guadalupe!
with much love :)

[signature]

THE BRIDGE BETWEEN THE EAST AND WEST:

A JOURNEY TO TRUTH THROUGH HIS LOVE

SAMIA MARY ZUMOUT

"SAMYA"

DEDICATION:

FOR THE GREATER GLORY OF GOD

IN HONOR OF:

MY EARTHLY FAMILY

My Loving and Faithful Parents: Sonia and Elias

My Amazing Brothers and Sister and their Families

All My Wonderful Relatives: Aunts, Uncles and Cousins

All My Incredible Friends

Joshua Ministries and PAHIES Prayer Group Members

Everyone who has Ever Prayed or will Pray for Me

Anyone who has Ever Crossed or will Cross my Path in Life

IN GRATITUDE FOR:

MY HEAVENLY FAMILY

The Holy Trinity
(Father, Son and Holy Spirit)

Blessed Mother Mary

My Guardian Angel (s)

All the Saints

All the Angels

TABLE OF CONTENTS

Foreword

This unusual book written by a unique personality offers the author's theories and views as a possible bridge between Middle Eastern and Western cultures since she lived and experienced both and knows whereof she speaks.

Drawn irresistibly to visit Medjugorje, Samia Zumout becomes a witness to two miracles and is involved in a shattering life-changing event. The love of God and our Lord Jesus' Blessed Mother become central in her life as she herself puts it: "Without God, my life has no meaning."

Zumout considers everyone her "sibling" and maintains that the love of God and one's fellowman is the only authentic bridge.

Thoughtfully written, intimately expressed, *The Bridge between the East and West* echoes the words of St. John: "See what love the Father has bestowed on us so that we may be called the children of God."

Martha Wilson
Widow, retired educator and mother of six children

Chapter One

God is Love

"Whoever is without love does not know God; for God is love."

\- 1 John 4: 8

I am not afraid to talk about God. God is the source of life and healing love in my life. This book is about that love. God **is** Love. What do you feel when you read these words? I will repeat them one more time.

God is Love.

Perhaps my words are making you feel angry right now. I have met many people over the years, including close friends, who are very angry with God and refuse to give Him a chance. They have suffered enormously in their lives so they feel betrayed by Him and cannot experience His love or protection when they need it the most. I truly understand their anger and empathize with them. I also have endured very difficult and dark periods. I have often found myself feeling angry with God, feeling abandoned by Him to the point of reaching despair; but through my life's journey, despite what I have endured, God has demonstrated that He *is* Love. He has confirmed to me that everything in my life - good and bad - has its purpose. As you read about my life, you may also realize, looking back in your own life, that you have not been abandoned by God either. My greatest hope for you is to find some answers to *your* life's questions through reading about mine. I pray that

1

my journey serves as an important step toward achieving inner-peace and healing for all my readers.

Maybe you are uncertain who God is, or, maybe you agree with me that God is Love; regardless, I welcome you to accompany me on this journey through my life to my own discovery of God and His abundant love for each of us. This book is for everyone who is willing to open his or her heart to experience God's healing love.

The purpose of this book is not to convert you or convince you of my *own* beliefs as I relate them to you. I am inviting you to join me as I share with you *my* spiritual journey so far in this life. It fashioned *my* beliefs and led me to live and experience God's immense and immeasurable love for me and for everyone else around me. My life's journey has stretched over several different continents, from Jordan in the Middle East, to the United States in the West and, hence, the first part of the title of my book "*The Bridge between the East and West.*" The "bridge" represents my life.

As I open my heart and share with you *my* life's journey toward God, I pray you will also try to open your heart as you read my story. I challenge you to step outside of your social paradigm that might have restricted your beliefs and open your soul to a new way of seeing things, a new meaning for life and your life's mission.

Prepare yourself to see the world through *my* eyes as I take you to other countries and introduce you to different cultures. Prepare to smile or even laugh. Prepare to feel some anger and sadness. Allow your tears to flow. Get ready to be *challenged* to look deeply within your own heart. I pray that by the time we conclude this journey together, you will be filled with more faith, more hope, more inner-peace, more joy, and most importantly, more LOVE.

WHAT IS LOVE?

Unfortunately, in today's world, the word "love" has lost its meaning. We use it for everything; I love these shoes, I love golf, I love my dog, I love my iPod, I love this movie, I love this song and I love sushi.

When I refer to God as being LOVE, I take this word very seriously; I would like to restore it to its original and full meaning. Unfortunately, throughout history, many have used God's name to destroy life and sow seeds of hatred, when in reality God is the heart of life and love.

My life's journey has showed me that LOVE entails forgiveness, sacrifice, mercy, compassion, hope, faith, trust, understanding, self-giving, healing, truth, vibrant life, peace and joy. These are a few of the words that describe God who is the essence of LOVE. Love is the heart of everything alive. Love is the core of our being. Love is the oxygen that is essential for our existence.

All the books in the world could never teach us about God or His love if we never had an intimate knowledge of Him. Once we actually experience His love and open our hearts to receive Him, we never remain the same. With love, God has changed my heart and has healed the woundedness that encompassed lies I believed about myself and my surroundings. Only God's truth dispels my false beliefs. Only His light dissipates the darkness in my heart. Only His love restores my life and transforms my wounded holes into wholeness.

Of course, whenever defining love, it feels natural to recall St. Paul's famous words about the characteristics of love that are so frequently read during Christian wedding ceremonies:

3

"Love is patient, love is kind. It is not jealous, [love] is not pompous, it is not inflated, it is not rude, it does not seek its own interests, it is not quick-tempered, it does not brood over injury, it does not rejoice over wrongdoing but rejoices with the truth. It bears all things, believes all things, hopes all things, endures all things. Love never fails."[1]

WHO AM I?

I am not a theologian or a historian and I certainly am not a therapist or a psychologist. By profession, I am a lawyer and also a real estate broker. I am very blessed that my life's journey has led me to become fluent in four languages, English, Arabic, Spanish and French. Through these blessings, God has allowed me to share His love with people of different cultures. My university degrees and what I do to earn my living do not define who I am as a human being. Any profession points only to one skill and everyone's life is in a constant change of motion. I now define myself by my relationship with the One who is the reason behind my existence on earth. He gives meaning to my life and everything that occurs in it. He is the One who has strategically planned my birth and my specific mission in life. He is the only One who knows the exact minute and even second when I will finally *graduate* from earth to my heavenly home. Of course, I have not always defined myself in this manner. God has proven to me He is my Heavenly Father in many ways throughout my life, particularly, in the midst of a horrific incident that could have traumatized me forever. I am first and foremost a daughter and a child of God, our Heavenly Father. You, the reader, are my spiritual brother or

---

[1] 1Corinthians 13: 4-8

sister and also a son or a daughter of our Heavenly Father, regardless of what creed, religious background or beliefs you may currently practice.

As you will read in later chapters, I experienced some extraordinary miraculous events that changed the course of my life and occurred while I was backpacking through Europe with some friends. My reasoning mind could not fathom what I witnessed with my eyes or experienced in my heart. My notion of God changed forever and I have been invited to share these powerful experiences throughout California and even Mexico.

Let us begin our journey as I welcome you to the country of my birth, our first destination.

Chapter Two

Growing Up in Jordan

"You formed my inmost being; you knit me in my mother's womb. I praise you, so wonderfully you made me; wonderful are your works! My very self you knew; my bones were not hidden from you, when I was being made in secret, fashioned as in the depths of the earth. Your eyes foresaw my actions; in your book all are written down; my days were shaped, before one came to be."

- Psalm 139: 13-16

I was born in Amman, the capital of Jordan, in October of 1969 and was raised there until the age of thirteen. The first language I learned was Arabic. I was born into a family that was - and always has been - Christian. My mother was raised Byzantine Catholic and my father Roman Catholic. I was baptized Roman Catholic and grew up embracing the rich teachings of these two arms of the Catholic Church, the Eastern and Western Rites.

Today, Christians in Jordan constitute approximately five percent (5%) of the population. Many Jordanian Christians belong to the Greek Orthodox Church, others to the Roman Catholic Church, some to the Eastern Catholic and some to the Protestant Church. The majority of the remaining ninety-five percent (95%) of the Jordanian population are Sunni Muslims.

Christians in the Middle East call themselves "Christians" regardless of their denominations. I was surprised after I immigrated to the United States to know that to many people's understanding, the word "Christian" implied "Protestant" which excluded Catholics and other denominations. Catholics are Christians. The word "catholic" means "universal." The Catholic Church refers to the universal church which was founded over 2000 years ago by Jesus Christ himself through his apostles when He said to Peter according to the Gospel of Matthew: *"And so I say to you, you are Peter, and upon this rock I will build my Church, and the gates of the netherworld shall not prevail against it. I will give you the keys to the kingdom of heaven. Whatever you bind on earth shall be bound in heaven; and whatever you loose on earth shall be loosed in heaven."*[2] Peter was the first Pope in the Roman Catholic Church.

As a child, I was taught to say my prayers every night before going to bed. Because of the restrictive nature of the work week in Jordan, my parents took me and my brothers to church on all major holidays such as Christmas, Holy Week celebrations and Easter. Since Jordan was a Muslim country, Sundays were regular workdays so both of my parents were required to work. Friday was the official Muslim holiday and this was the only day off for people then. Fortunately, my house in Jordan was located right across the street from a Byzantine Catholic church. I got up every Sunday and went to church by myself. Even at an early age of seven, I would wake up early, completely on my own and make it to the 7:30 am Liturgy or Mass service.

---

[2] Matthew 16: 18-19

Looking back, I am amazed at the inner drive and hunger I had for God which surpassed my limited understanding at the time. I have come to know that God's gentle love was present then and has always guided my footsteps in my journey toward Him.

I was raised in a conservative home centered upon high morals and very strong family ties and values. My parents taught me the importance of family unity at a very young age. Family was at the heart of everything. My paternal grandparents had lived with my family ever since I was born. In Jordan, it was customary for the oldest male son to care for his elderly parents by taking them into his own household since it was unthinkable to place parents in a convalescent home. Children were raised to respect the elderly in a very special and tender way.

I grew up with two older brothers, Nabil and Ramzi. The three of us were born in three consecutive years and often played together and shared the same neighborhood friends whom we treated as family. We played the same games that children around the world play, such as, hide-and-seek, Monopoly, Scrabble, chess, football (soccer), basketball, tennis, ping-pong, badminton, and often played with and traded our marbles.

Both of my parents came from very large families so I was always surrounded by aunts, uncles, and many cousins who were like my own siblings. Casual family get-togethers were always filled with a variety of delicious food, loud conversations, singing, dancing and much love and laughter. In general, the Jordanian culture was centered on the family and the social events that revolved around it. People in Jordan were inner-connected through very strong community ties and obligations as they pulled together in joyful occasions and sad ones, such as, birthdays, anniversaries, religious holidays, births, baptisms, graduations, pre-wedding parties, weddings, post-wedding parties, going-away parties, coming-back parties, illness, death and funerals.

Nevertheless, growing up in Jordan not only as a Christian but also as a female was often difficult for me on multiple levels. I grew up dealing with issues that caused me to feel a tremendous awareness about myself, my femininity, my religious orientation, my gender and even my darker, olive-skinned complexion. Many Jordanians had light-skinned color and a lighter-skinned complexion was considered to be better, prettier or more upper class. Although I was born in Jordan and my father was Jordanian, my mother was Palestinian-Lebanese. My father had met and married her in Beirut - the capitol city of Lebanon - while he was studying at the university but once they were married, they moved to Jordan. We often went back to Lebanon to visit my maternal grandparents and family during summer vacations, Christmas, Easter Holidays and I had the opportunity to live in Beirut for two years when I was very young. Incidentally, I greatly enjoyed going to Lebanon where things seemed to be different. I felt a sense of freedom and cultural openness that I yearned for when I returned to Jordan. I also felt extremely blessed by the love I received from my mother's family - grandparents, aunts, uncles, and cousins.

I recall various childhood memories in Jordan where other people's reaction to my religion made me feel like there was something wrong with me. For example, during the first seven years of my academic life, I attended an excellent private school. It was acclaimed for teaching French - besides Arabic and English - and was known to be the best in the country. It had very high academic standards and requirements. The school was owned by a

Christian family and was very well-known in the capital city of Amman. Both Christian and Muslim children attended this school. Like any child my age, I wanted to make friends, to be accepted, to be liked and to feel like I belonged. Unfortunately, I recall various incidents which made me feel otherwise and led me to feel ashamed of whom I was. This usually occurred when I met the parents of my Muslim friends while playing or visiting at their homes. I just dreaded the much-too-familiar question I anticipated with so much uneasiness and anxiety: *"Are you Muslim or Christian?"*

These words always tore through my ears like a sharp knife and repeatedly punctured my fragile young heart. I do not know how I managed to hide my tears during those moments as I knew too well the usual consequences of my response which sometimes led to either the loss of my friend's companionship or a change in his or her behavior toward me. As a child, I was incapable of processing these emotions; I did what most children usually did when feeling tremendous shame, I internalized everything and tried to block them somewhere in the back of my mind. I did not want to feel different. I wanted to belong and to feel loved and accepted by my peers. Perhaps you can also identify with some of these feelings.

My religion was not something I could hide or escape from, as even my passport identified it. Christians in Jordan were often referred to on television in Muslim religious programs and amongst many people in the society as "infidels." Christians were treated inferiorly although nobody publicly talked about that or dared to admit it. We were considered to have a western religion since the majority of the people toward the west of the Middle East were Christians. Ironically, Jesus Christ was born precisely in the Middle East and Christianity spread from there to the West and then to the rest of the world. Many people around the world today seem to forget that historical detail. They are surprised to know there are Christian Arabs in the Middle East. The religion of Islam did not come into existence until the seventh century. This was over 600 years after Christ was crucified. Christianity was widespread by then. Even after the rapid expansion of Islam from the seventh century onwards through the Islamic conquests, many Christians, who survived the persecutions, chose not to convert to Islam. They maintained their Christian beliefs. To practice their religion, they were forced to pay a special tax in exchange for their safety and freedom of worship. Many others converted to Islam to avoid paying the levied tax.

Like Arab Muslims and Arab Jews, Arab Christians also refer to God as "*Allah,*" since this is the word for "God" in Arabic.

I learned at a very young age in Jordan that to keep the peace and stay alive, there were two subjects that I should never talk about or discuss publicly: politics or religion. As you know, being a minority is never a pleasant thing. Growing up as a Christian and also a female in a Muslim country probably produced some of the deepest wounds of my heart. This might not be the experience of every Christian who grew up or is still growing up there today. I know I am only one voice, but nevertheless, it is *my* voice and *my* experience.

Although I was raised in Jordan with a Christian upbringing, I cannot honestly say I ever truly experienced God or His love in my heart. It was not until much later in life I found a *personal* relationship with our Lord Jesus Christ. My knowledge of God was an intellectual knowledge based on what I was taught in my Catholic family, things I memorized in my religious education class at my Catholic Middle School and also based on the stringent cultural views of God that were entrenched in my mind. In Jordan, as in most other Arabic-speaking countries in the Middle East, the culture was very much dominated by the Islamic religious views and values.

Growing up, my image of God was that of a very distant, strict, detached, mostly angry, and unforgiving God who was out to punish me for every mistake I made. The fear and wrath of God were instilled in me as they were instilled in many people. As children, we learned, in the society, to do things out of "fear" of God instead of out of "love" for God. We often heard as children the pronouncement *"God will punish you for doing that!"*

Fear and unfortunately shame seemed to be the driving forces for the majority of the things we did or did not do. As a young girl, fear and shame were embedded in me in such a profound way that I sometimes felt like I carried not only my share but also the share of some women from generations before me.

Just to clarify, there are two types of shame that I have been able to identify. One type is actually positive and healthy as it makes us feel bad when we do something wrong or we behave inappropriately. This healthy shame also reminds us of our human limitations and dependency on our Creator, God. The second type of shame that I am referring to here is mainly the poisonous shame that gets injected into our minds through the judgments of others and also through our own self-judgment, making us feel defective, inherently flawed, inferior, unworthy and unlovable. In fact, expressions such as *"shame on you"* or *"that is shameful"* were very common daily sayings that I and most young girls were accustomed to hearing. Sometimes the most innocent things I did as young girl brought me shame, such as, riding a bicycle, wearing short skirts, befriending someone from the opposite sex or even mentioning the word "sex."

By far, the worst shaming crime a girl or a young woman could commit was to "dishonor" herself or her family by losing her virginity out of wedlock. A girl's entire "honor" and "value" was connected to her "virginity." Of course, this rule only applied to females while males were completely exempt from it. A double-standard between men and women was accepted as normal and nobody dared to question or challenge this inequality. In fact, following a wedding night, many families then (and I believe this practice still applies in some families today) wanted to see tangible evidence that the bride had been a virgin on her wedding night - such as a towel with fresh blood stains to indicate her hymen had still been intact.

As I write these lines, I cannot help a nauseous feeling in my stomach that a woman's value could be degraded and demeaned to this extent. How is it possible that most of the people in Jordan, and similar cultures, accept the notion that a woman's honor is attached to her "hymen"? How could her principles, integrity, intellect, personality, education and aspirations in life, much less – her life, count for nothing? Some girls, *even innocent victims of rape*, have been slaughtered by their own fathers, brothers, or cousins in the name of "honor." This act is referred to as "honor killing." I am astonished that good, educated and reasonable people, men and women alike, accept this barbaric practice without question.

I have come to learn that my honor as a woman will never be defined only by a "thin membrane" in my body. It is defined and anointed by my relationship with our Heavenly Father who has ordained my life and my purpose. Our entire bodies, both male and female, are created *sacred* by God. We are the temples of God's Holy Spirit who dwells within us,[3] giving us life and men and women alike are all called to live chaste lives within marriage and without marriage. We are God's precious and unique creation. Nothing we do can deny us the honor of being His beloved children. As His children on earth, nothing that we do, whether pure or sinful, will change this truth! We will always be His children and He will always be our forgiving and loving Heavenly Father and Creator. He will never stop loving us. It is against His nature. I cannot help but recall our Lord Jesus' words to the Scribes and Pharisees who brought him a woman who had been caught in adultery. They wanted to test him by inquiring whether they should follow the law and stone her to death. Jesus' truthful and vindicating response left them with no choice but to silently walk away one by one, beginning with the elders. He said: *"Let the one among you who is without sin be the first to throw a stone at her."*[4] After that, Jesus did not condemn the woman but asked her not to sin anymore.[5]

Just as prisoners were bound by shackles to restrict their freedom, culture in the majority of Middle Eastern countries seems to bind people, especially girls and young women, with shame to constrain their growth, their self-determination and their free will. Ultimately, it was about control. I believe that shame was passed on generationally and has been used by the devil as a major weapon to separate us from God's love. If our false belief

---

[3] 1 Corinthians 6: 19-20
[4] John 8:7
[5] John 8:11

system told us that we were inherently defective and unlovable, then it was only logical to believe that we were unworthy of God's love.

Despite these negative aspects that I just have mentioned, there are many aspects that I truly value and enjoy in the Jordanian culture, such as the generous self-giving hospitality of the Jordanians, the strong family ties, the frequent family get-togethers, the closeness of the extended family and the caring community feeling.

Ironically, because of the family and cultural closeness, many individuals lose their true identity and their true calling in life. I do not know of all the changes in today's Jordanian society, however, when I was growing up, there was no such thing as individual freedom of choice, which was the freedom to decide for oneself what one wanted to do or to become. For the most part, the family – both immediate and extended - and even the society at large had a say in how the individual would develop, who and when this individual should marry, how this individual should dress or behave in public and how this individual should think. The list goes on and on. The individual in many cases had no choice because all the choices were dictated by the family or by the culture. Families were so absorbed in their social reputation that a person often heard the expression *"what will people say?"* This served as a guilt-ridden condemnation of almost any act an individual dared make which might not have coincided with the rules of society. For example, many families pressured their sons to become engineers or doctors. Society highly praised such professions. Parents felt proud to be called the "parents of" an engineer or a doctor. Due to the high number of such professions, the small country was saturated with unemployed and unfulfilled engineers who eventually changed professions or became taxi drivers. Even the educational system in Jordan required students to choose their field of study and determine their life's course as early as thirteen years of age. In addition, it was a cultural norm to marry young in Jordan. Older women were shunned and pitied for being unmarried at twenty-three years of age since a single woman's value in the Middle East decreased with age. Many people compromised personal happiness and freedom in order to adhere to cultural expectations. Appearances were extremely important.

Amazingly, this exercise of control over another individual's life was usually done in the name of "love." It was "out of love" that a family did this to their son or daughter. If a person had the courage to question these cultural norms that dictated their life, then this person was compelled to feel very guilty, very ashamed and was severely condemned by the family for being disrespectful of his or her elders. It was not within the cultural norms to question or challenge the status quo and naming this status quo "love" led to a false belief about what "love" really is!

I did not doubt such families intended to "love" their son or daughter. This was the only way they knew how to show love and the only way they themselves had been shown love. This is precisely where I take a stand and challenge the meaning of this incredible word "love." Is this type of love supportive and nurturing of the other person? Does it foster an environment of trust and growth? Is this a self-giving love or is it a selfish and self-seeking love? Does this love truly reflect God, who is the *essence* and *source* of all love?

Sadly, sometimes the Jordanian culture felt like a double-edged sword to me. One side gave me a sense of family and community. The other side stripped me of my freedom, the right to be myself, to be loved just as I was -

the child that God created me to be. It seemed to me that an individual's identity too often had to be connected to someone else's identity.

For example, who I was in the society as a person was connected to what my family's last name was, what my religion was, who my father was and what his profession was. My father's identity was also connected to what his last name was, his profession, his education and the name of his first-born male son. The identity of almost all fathers and mothers in Jordan automatically changed as soon as they had their first-born male son. Their names suddenly changed to the title "father of" and "mother of" followed by the name of their son.

Let's take a father named "Jim" and a mother named "Jennifer." They had a first-born son whom they called "Sam." After Sam's birth, people will start calling Jim and Jennifer with their new names "father of Sam" and "mother of Sam" (in Jordanian Arabic dialect, it would be "*Abu* Sam" and "*Um* Sam.") In the event that these parents only had baby girls and no boys, the parents would be called by their original first names. It was not common practice to contemplate the potential emotional damage that this inflicted on the other siblings in the family, the remaining brothers and sisters. Of course, this practice insinuates that the remaining children are less important than the first-born male. Somehow most people in the society accepted this old tradition, took pride in it and did not question it.

As I contemplated writing about this subject, I could not help but wonder about the possible consequences I might face in the future as a result of "speaking out" or "breaking the silence" and choosing to no longer submit to the familiar cultural denial. Writing this book would come at a price. How would my family and extended family react to my expressed words? Would I lose any of my Middle Eastern friends? Would I be shunned by the American Middle Eastern community that knows me? What would the possible consequences be?

As a young girl, feeling afraid and voiceless was as natural to me as playing with dolls. Now, as an adult, I want to live in freedom and without fears. My Lord Jesus Christ taught that *"the truth will set you free."*[6] I want to live in truth and enjoy the freedom that results from this truth no matter how bad the consequences may be. The truth may be painful at first, but believe it or not, it takes much more effort to live in denial and deception.

As I continue to share my life's journey, you might experience a range of emotions depending on your own country, origins or culture. Please note that my intention is *not* to anger you or to make you hate anyone from Jordan, the Middle East, Muslims or any other group of people. Actually, I have many close friends who are Muslims and also who are Arabs. I tremendously value their friendship and respect them immensely. We have shared many wonderful times together filled with laughter, supportive love, great conversations, dancing and of course a lot of delicious food. In fact one of my best friends, Rasmiya, is Muslim and I love her dearly. God has used her friendship during many crucial moments of my life as He often spoke to me through her words or gestures. We have been friends for over thirteen years and she is like a sister to me. We have shared many moments of laughter as well as tears and many profound conversations and reflections on God.

In order for you to understand where I am today in my life's journey, you have to know where I have been and how I progressed and grew along

---

[6] John 8:32

the path. Looking back at the painful experiences in my past, I realized those painful moments were the catalyst to my spiritual awakening. I am thankful for *each* detail of my past and would *not* change any of it, even if I could. Our Lord is teaching me that the painful periods of our lives can become the gateways to our purification and spiritual growth, if we willingly turn them to Him. They can commit us to seeking the *truth* in life and thereby finding God.

As I will thoroughly discuss in later chapters, through my inner-healing experiences, our Lord has healed my heart of most of these hurtful memories which enables me now to open my heart to you without feeling any shame, resentment or anger. I hope that through my journey, your heart will also find some of the healing it might need, regardless of your creed, religion or beliefs. I know that you also have your own story and journey. I am certain that some of my pain might feel familiar to you although it might look different or have been inflicted in a different manner. The more I allow God's love to heal my wounded heart, the more I am able to have compassion toward myself and others, especially the ones who caused me the most hurt. True forgiveness comes from God's infinite love and graces. I pray that your experience will be similar to mine. It has taken many years for my mind and heart to finally be able to identify with and comprehend what the Lord Jesus said while dying on the cross: *"Father, forgive them, they know not what they do."*[7]

---

[7] Luke 23:34

Chapter Three

Finding my New Home in America

"For I know well the plans I have in mind for you, says the Lord, plans for your welfare, not for woe plans to give you a future full of hope."
- Jeremiah 29:11

In Jordan, I often heard my father talk about immigrating to another country. For a while he talked about England, then Germany and finally the United States of America. I did not take him seriously until the year 1981 when he finally planned a flight to the United States to visit his cousin and explore the immigration option. My father wanted a better life for his family and his three children. He knew that eventually we would travel abroad to pursue our university education. My parents instilled in us at a very early age the value of higher education. My father wanted his family to stay together, as most of the young adults who studied abroad never returned to their country. He found a good immigration lawyer who helped him to obtain the lawful permanent residence card ("Green Card") through business channels for himself and the whole family. Before we knew it, the doors opened up for us and my mother was diligently selling our properties in Jordan and packing up our personal belongings in preparation for our imminent immigration.

On Wednesday, July 13, 1983, my life changed dramatically, and forever. It was a day I will never forget. I clearly remember the darkness outside as we got up before the crack of dawn. I tearfully carried my suitcases to the street where our neighbors, also tearful, waited to bid us farewell prior to our departure to the airport. These neighbors were like family to us. We grew up together, played together, had meals together and shared many wonderful memories. It was so hard for me to believe that I might never see them again. Immigration is never easy because it entails starting all over in a strange new place, with a new language, new culture, new school, new foods and new surroundings. In time, the immigrant makes new friends, finds new neighbors, and even a new extended family, but the loss of what is left behind stays in the heart.

So many questions raced through my head. Will I be able to adjust? Will I be able to move forward and assimilate into a new culture? Will people understand my accent? Will I understand them if they speak too fast? Will I be able to make new friends? Will I be accepted? Will I fit in?

I was thirteen years old and I knew I was leaving so much behind. I had many relatives, cousins, aunts, uncles and close friends. Despite some of the pain and hurt that life in Jordan had caused my heart, I had become accustomed to it and did not want to leave. It is sometimes much easier to stay in a familiar state of pain instead of taking the chance to face the fear of the unknown, no matter how liberating the outcome might be. Furthermore, when we are completely immersed in something, we do not realize how influential it is on our heart and soul until we finally leave it. For example, it is hard to know that we are in a dark room if we have never experienced light before. We conform to the darkness, as it is the only thing we know, and we learn to adjust to it, feel our way around it and adapt to it. Once we experience the light and we are able to compare it to the darkness we previously accepted, it would be hard to go back to tolerating that darkness.

We arrived at San Francisco International Airport where we were greeted by my father who had moved to Sacramento, California, after he received his Green Card because he liked the city's quiet life and the climate was similar to Jordan's. As we drove from San Francisco to Sacramento, I was fascinated by the beauty of the buildings in downtown San Francisco, the green and luscious nature along the way and how everyone drove in such an orderly fashion on the wide highways. I was impressed that nobody honked their car horn as they drove. You see, in Jordan, honking the horn while driving was as natural as breathing. Despite the deep sadness I was feeling, I started to become excited about the possibilities and adventures in this new country which quickly became my home.

What I loved the most about living in the United States was how easily everything seemed to run. I did not need to bribe anyone to take care of normal business. I just took a number, stood in line and within minutes someone attended to me. People actually stood in line and did not pile up in front of a window or cut in front of me. My parents did not need to know someone or have an "inside connection" to get their driver's licenses. There was a structure to getting things done. People naturally respected the system and adhered to it, which produced order.

I also quickly noticed that drivers even respected the street signs. The "Stop" sign was an effective and obeyed signal. People fully stopped and did not just run through it while honking on their horns as if the sign was merely a street decoration. I think many immigrants to this country, or Americans who lived in the Middle East or Latin America, can relate to my observations and are hopefully smiling while reading this.

When I walked down the street, I noticed that men did not stare at me or make cat sounds or hissing sounds like I was used to hearing back in Jordan. I actually felt respected when I walked. I did not feel like an object. Everyone seemed to mind his or her own business. My adjustment to this life was easy.

My parents enrolled me and my two older brothers in high school. I started as a freshman. I was amazed by how friendly everyone was at the school. I quickly made friends and joined the tennis and basketball teams as well as many academic and social clubs. Things were different but thankfully I adjusted rapidly. I was able to assimilate easily into the new culture and the new language. Although I spoke English prior to arriving in the United States, I was taught the British dialect. I learned many new American expressions and lost most of my accent in a very short period of time.

Within three months, I felt fully adjusted. Nobody ever asked me about my religion or my belief system. My friends just accepted me the way I was. Some were curious to know about Jordan and others had not ever heard of it. Some friends had the typical stereotypes about Arabs in their heads, based on what they had seen in Hollywood movies, such as people living in tents, riding camels and covered women everywhere. I often had to explain that I rode the bus to school, lived in a regular house and wore western clothes. Only very religious Muslim women covered their heads or faces. We had similar things that people had here, cars, houses and televisions.

One thing that struck me in a powerful way was the high rate of divorce in the families of my friends. When I lived in Jordan, divorce was unheard of and was socially unacceptable. I did not know anyone who was divorced. Talking to my new friends in school, they often made reference to their mom's boyfriend, or their dad's girlfriend or their step-parents. This was something entirely new to me and it took a while to understand.

Despite my rapid adjustment to my new country and home, I did face some difficult challenges. Although I made many friends, it was very hard for them to relate to me and the conservative culture from which I had come. For example, they could not understand why I could not stay out late, spend the night at their homes, or go out to parties with them. It made no sense to them why I was not allowed to have a boyfriend or date anyone. To them, it was natural for everyone in high school to do those things. Sometimes I just grew weary of explaining myself and my culture. In Jordan, dating was never an option, neither in high school nor the university. My parents were very conservative; I had to be obedient to their values and rules, regardless of my age. What made it worse was trying to explain and justify some cultural things that I didn't agree with myself.

Another challenging matter for me then, and even today, was the way people mispronounced my first name: "Samia." Although it is not a familiar name in America, it is actually a very common name in the Middle East. The name "Samia" is an Arabic word which means "sublime" or "the exalted one."

I do not know why, but many people here have a hard time pronouncing it, which has caused me much anguish for over twenty-four years. I know you might be thinking that it is a bit silly for me to suffer over this. If you take into consideration that my name is what everyone calls me to get my attention, and I have to live with it 24 hours a day, then you might understand my pain. My name is the symbol of my identity. Having it mispronounced makes me feel disconnected from the person calling me. In fact, there is a strong possibility that at this instant your mind is mispronouncing my name as you are reading these paragraphs. It would really mean a lot to my heart if you can say it correctly. Would you allow me to teach you how to pronounce it? It is two syllables: "Sam" and "ya." It is pronounced similarly to the names Sonya or Tanya, only you replace the first syllable with "Sam" and get "Sam-ya." I know I probably should have changed the spelling of my name twenty-four years ago to "Samya" but it was already written as "Samia" on all my legal documents and therefore I felt like I just needed to live with it. If you are wondering about the pronunciation of my last name, let's not even open that can of worms. Saying my first name correctly makes me extremely happy and is more than sufficient for now.

Getting back to my story, in 1983, my parents opened and operated a Middle Eastern restaurant in Sacramento. I helped them after school, on the weekends and summer vacations. Although we had left the Middle Eastern culture in Jordan, I felt like we walked into another one in Sacramento. Many of our clients were either Middle Eastern university students or members of the Arab-American community.

The desire of my heart was to feel "free," just to be myself and have my own thoughts, beliefs and convictions. I wanted to discover myself and who I truly was. Because I went back to living within a "cultural system" it was hard for me to be authentic as I had to conform to the behavioral expectations of others. It was as if everyone else around me was my judge. In fact, I noticed that even my own parents became stricter with me here than they were in Jordan. In a way, I could understand how they, like most other immigrant parents, wanted to make sure I did not go "wild" with all the freedoms this country offered.

On one hand, I felt like I was worse off here than I was in Jordan because my freedom was more restricted. On the other hand, working in this restaurant enabled me to meet other open-minded Arab-Americans who came from all over the Middle East. It felt very refreshing for me to feel understood and connected to others who shared my feelings and even some of my hurts and concerns. I made some very close friendships that continue to this day. One friend in particular, Wendy, has been like a sister to me for over twenty-four years. In many ways, she has been a priceless treasure from God because she has accompanied me through a significant portion of my journey, especially the difficult periods.

My parents quickly joined and became actively involved in a local Catholic Byzantine Church. My whole family started attending the Sunday Liturgy services. I felt great being able to practice my religion and faith without any fears. For the first time in my life, I felt like I belonged as a Christian. I took classes to become a Sunday school teacher for the children and taught for one year, which was wonderful. I felt reconnected to my faith, although it was mainly an intellectual experience and not an intimate one with God. I knew my faith through my head, but I had not yet experienced God in my heart. Although I recited my daily prayers, I only made my daily *speech* to Him and did not converse with Him. Nevertheless, that experience still taught me a lot about God. It served as a basis for the deeper connection I made with Him in the coming years. I know now that the journey from my *head* to my *heart* was the longest journey to make.

In 1987, when I was about to graduate from Encina High School, something wonderful happened to my family. My sister Sophie was born. Of course, the initial news of my mom's pregnancy was very shocking to me as I was sixteen years old and the youngest in the family. Many people thought my parents were crazy to have another child, especially when they were in their early to mid-forties with three adult children. Nevertheless, Sophie's birth was one of the best things that ever happened to us. She was a marvelous gift from God.

I admired my parents tremendously for not falling prey to the medical field and society's pressures to have an abortion. I also esteemed them for being great witnesses, of the power of their faith and trust in God and His will in their lives to everyone who knew them. They silently taught me by their example. They knew well that all children were God's precious gifts to their parents and that God would take care of them. There is a very wise adage in Arabic that says: *"Each child is from God and comes into to the world bringing his own blessings."* This saying is very true to me. My parents did not have the financial means to have another child. They were trying to support my two older brothers, who were already in universities, and myself, who was about to begin college. They remained faithful and the Lord provided for them and their daily needs. My sister Sophie was born into our family and brought many blessings.

I feel very grateful to God for blessing me with a devoted, loving earthly family. In addition to my wonderful little sister Sophie, I have been blessed with two amazing older brothers and none of us have suffered from "sibling rivalry." I am very grateful for the unconditional love and support that I have always received from them and I love each of them with all my heart.

Because of the anticipated birth of my sister, in my senior year of high school I decided to apply to the University of California at Davis which was a great local university. I wanted to go to a university that was close to my parent's house so that I could drive home on the weekends and watch my sister grow. I had never had a sister before and I did not want to miss out on experiencing her blossoming and becoming her own person.

I attended UC Davis from 1987 through 1992 and graduated with a double-major in International Relations and French. These two bachelor degrees did not reflect the range of knowledge I gained through my university of life experience and through the amazing people I met from all over the world, who taught me so much. These were some of the best days of my life.

During my first year, I lived in the university dormitory sharing a three-bedroom suite with five wonderful women. One of them, Andrea, became a very close friend of mine. We were roommates for three of the following four years. God used Andrea in a powerful way to change the course of my life.

Andrea and I hit it off right away. She was a self-giving person with a truly wonderful and compassionate heart. Her father was from Argentina and her mother was American. As a result, Andrea was fluent in both English and Spanish. I loved talking to her as I enjoyed her open-mindedness about other cultures. We enjoyed discussing almost all subjects with the exception of one: God. Whenever we talked about God, we often ended having horrible arguments. Andrea was agnostic at the time. Looking back, I think we both were immature spiritually; we just did not know it. I was arguing with her about someone whom I knew intellectually but truly did not know intimately.

On the other hand, I believe that her own rejection of God was based on the painful religious persecutions that her ancestors had endured, during World War II, which led them to either deny God or dismiss Him completely. (I did not know this at the time, but I learned of it several years later, which made me understand her better and have more compassion for her.) So we both knew that in order for us to guard our friendship, we needed to avoid discussing the subject of God.

During our second year of college, Andrea strongly encouraged me to apply for the Education Abroad Program. This was an exchange program organized by the University of California where students who applied and were accepted would spend their junior year (or third year) studying at a foreign university. The university credits would be transferable back to their local university. Since Andrea spoke Spanish fluently, she was applying for the program in Spain. Andrea had a burning desire to experience living outside of the United States. She asked me to apply for the program in France since I spoke French. She suggested taking the train and traveling throughout Europe for a month after we both finished our studies in Spain and France.

At first, I thought that Andrea had lost her mind. She knew how conservative my family was. I could not imagine that my father would ever allow me to go abroad to study alone for one full year. I was not even allowed to date or have a boyfriend although I was in college. I lived only twenty miles away from Sacramento which was within my parents' radar. Every time I drove back and forth from Sacramento to Davis, I needed to call my father to tell him that I arrived safely.

Andrea planted the seed in my head. I had a feeling deep within my heart that I was meant to participate in this program although I knew it would take a real miracle for my parents to consent. I began the lengthy application process. I thought to myself that most likely I would not be accepted into the program since there was a very rigorous selection and interview process. I convinced myself that if I applied and did not get to go to France, I would not have any regrets. I would know that it was not because I did not try or because my family refused to let me go, but because the program had declined me.

In anticipation of going to France to study, I applied to take my U.S. Citizenship examination having already been a legal resident for five years. It was amazing how fast the response from the Immigration and Naturalization Service was. Usually the process took many months or years, however, I heard back from them within several weeks and I was scheduled to take my oral exam and interview. I took the examination and passed. Several weeks later I was called for the swearing-in ceremony so that I could receive my naturalization certificate. I officially became a United States citizen on December 13, 1988. This was another crucial day in my life that I will never forget. I felt such a sense of pride and joy in the midst of my happy tears. Everything seemed like a dream. Thankfully, I was wide awake and my life was very real. After several months of fulfilling the application requirements that concluded with a two-hour interview with several professors from the French Department, I received the congratulatory letter that I was accepted! Andrea also was accepted and she was ecstatic. I did not know whether I should be jumping with joy or crying hysterically. Now that I was accepted, I did not know how to ask my parents. I felt like I had a huge mountain to climb without any gear or preparation.

I went to church, dropped on my knees and begged God for help. I did not know what to do. I had a strong feeling within my heart that there was an important reason for me to participate in this program. I could not explain the feeling; it was something that overwhelmed my understanding. So I asked God that if it was His divine will for me to go to France to study, He needed to give me a sign by softening my father's heart and facilitating the approval process. If my father resisted and declined, then I would understand that this was not God's will for me and the matter would be eternally closed. The deadline for the deposit submission was rapidly approaching so I decided to talk to my parents during that Sunday's lunch after church.

I still recall how anxious and nervous I was. I took with me a full file of supporting documentation ready to be presented to my parents. I had my entire argument outlined in my head about the benefits of this program, how it would help my degree in French and also in International Relations, how it would enhance my chances of getting admitted to law school later on, how Andrea was also going, how this program was part of the UC Davis program and thus was very closely monitored and how this program was not going to cost me any additional money. The tuition that I would pay would be identical to what I paid in California.

On Sunday, when my parents were sitting around the table eating lunch, my heart was beating so fast that I thought it was going to explode out of my chest. I told my parents that I needed to tell them something. I remember clearly my father's gaze as he was waiting for me to give him what might have appeared to be some bad news. Of course I was not direct in telling them. I started by talking about the program in general and how incredible it was and beneficial to anyone who would participate. Before I was able to complete my introductory statement and delve deeper into my presentation, my father suddenly interrupted me. He asked if this program would be beneficial for my university degrees. I hastily responded affirmatively. I told him that it would be valuable for both of my majors and might even expedite the time that it would take me to complete both degrees. My father became quiet, paused for a second and told me in a very peaceful manner the following unforgettable words:

"You know what is best for you Samia, if this will help your education and career, then I don't mind if you go. Do what is best for you."

I was completely stunned! I had no idea how I managed not to drop off my chair. I had not even gone through the introductory part of my argument and I already had my father's blessing and approval. This was too good to be true, almost too surreal. This was not the father that I thought I knew. Suddenly, I recalled my prayer in church and the sign I asked for. At that moment, I had no doubt in my mind and my heart that something big was awaiting me during the year that I would be overseas. My heart was overjoyed and I was very thankful to God.

Andrea and I started our preparations for our year abroad. We sat together and carefully planned the one-month backpacking trip. We decided that after our school year ended, we would meet, in June 1990, in France and travel by train to Italy, Greece, Crete, Czechoslovakia, Germany, Austria and finally back to France prior to returning to the United States. We were happy and excited. After all, traveling through Europe was one of our motivations to study abroad for the year. The plan was set in stone, or at least that was what we thought at the time. In August 1989, Andrea flew to Madrid, Spain and I flew to Lyon, France. We were ready to start our academic junior year abroad.

Chapter Four

Studying in France

"In his mind a man plans his course, but the Lord directs his steps."

- Proverbs 16:9

I flew into France on a hot summer day in August of 1989. Watching Paris from the plane's window was a dream come true. When I started studying French in Jordan at the age of four, I never imagined that one day I would be speaking it on a daily basis. I always loved how romantic the French language sounded and wished that I would become fluent in it.

Along with twenty-five other University of California students, I was welcomed at the Paris Charles de Gaulle International Airport by the program's director and his assistant. They cheerfully greeted us and took us to our temporary residence until we completed an orientation of two weeks. Everything was very well-planned and organized. We toured Paris for several days and took classes on French culture. We then headed to Lyon, a city in central France, where I would live and study for one year.

In Lyon, I became good friends with the other American students from the various University of California ("UC") campuses. They came from UCLA, UC Berkeley, UC Riverside, UC San Diego, UC Irvine, and, of course, UC Davis. We were all going through the same experience and enjoying the different culture, with a different language and customs, and different educational system. I was able to adjust very quickly since it was not my first time experiencing cultural changes.

In fact, I became very close friends with five other women from the program who made my year in France extra special. It happened that three of these women were also studying at UC Davis although I had never met them before. We truly had an unforgettable year. Throughout the year, we traveled together in France and also to other countries such as Switzerland, Belgium and Holland. We shared countless laughs and cries together.

I lived in Lyon with a very nice French family. I also made some great French friends at the university. I had many challenges too, especially the first three months. Although I started studying French at a very young age, I was amazed how different French sounded in France. People seemed to speak extremely fast, use a lot of jargon, and swallow half the syllables in their words. I went home every evening with a massive headache. I had to concentrate so hard during the day just to understand half the sentences or at least the context of what they were saying. I was glad that my other American friends were also feeling the same way. Fortunately, as the days went by, things improved very quickly. Before long, I was dreaming in French. That was when I knew I was adjusting to life in France.

On a side note, the constant smoking was something to which I could never adjust. I was not a smoker and never have been. It seemed that the majority of people in France were addicted to cigarettes. They smoked anytime, everywhere and anywhere. When I got home, my hair, my clothes and even my socks smelt like smoke. There was no such thing as a "nonsmoking" area. I really missed and greatly appreciated the laws about this addiction in the United States.

A different emotionally challenging issue for me while living in France was facing the question that I was frequently asked:

"Where are you from?"

My usual reply was:

"I am from the United States. I am American."

I was actually very proud to answer that, especially that I had become an American citizen the prior year. It seemed that my response was not sufficient as it was often followed by the following question:

*"Where are you **really** from?"*

The people who asked me this question could tell by looking at me that I had Middle Eastern features. We were speaking in French so it was not my slight English accent that might have made them assume I was not an American citizen.

This series of questions often troubled my heart. When I was naturalized as an American citizen in 1988, I was very ecstatic. You see, that was the first time in my life when I felt I belonged and had a country I could call "home." I was accepted just the way I was regardless of my religion, way of thinking, olive skin color and even my accent. I thought that I never had to deal again with trying to define or explain myself. These questions forced me to look at myself, especially my ethnic background, and think about who I was. For a while I struggled to define my identity. Eventually, I realized after much contemplation, that I did not need to restrict myself to one strict definition. The beautiful and unique characteristic of the American culture is that it embraces with open and generous arms everyone from all cultural

36

backgrounds. That is why it has been called the "melting pot." I realized I was blessed that my new country of citizenship allowed me to retain the things that I cherished from my previous culture and to discard the things that I opposed.

During the year in France, I was very active. Besides attending the university where I mainly studied political science and French literature, I was able to find two part-time jobs teaching English. One job was at a kindergarten school where I worked an hour each day. I really enjoyed this job as I loved children and was able to meet some very precious kids who helped me with my French as I taught them English. Another job, which I performed with a close American friend of mine, Sara, whom I met on the program, was teaching "business English" at an engineering university. What was great about this job was that it enabled us to make friends with students our age. They took us out in the city of Lyon and invited us to their dinners and get-togethers.

Incidentally, my friend Sara happened to be Jewish. When we first met in France, we initially were unsure how to behave with each other. The fact that she was Jewish and I was of Jordanian descent was significant. Neither of us had ever had a close friend from a country or religion that was historically considered as an "enemy." Sara had lived in Israel for one summer which made her more familiar with the conflict. As you probably know from watching the news or reading the newspapers, Arabs – particularly Palestinians - and Israelis have been in a horrific conflict for many years. As a young child in Jordan, I was taught that Jews were the enemy. Probably, many Jews in Israel were also taught that Arabs were the enemy. Unfortunately, this blind hatred is very deeply-rooted. It is built on fear, suspicion and total mistrust that neither side dares to question out of fear of being considered weak or a traitor.

Amazingly, Sara and I developed a very deep friendship that has continued today. We both learned so much from each other. Our friendship showed us that in so many ways we were so alike and wanted the same things from life. We both wanted to live in peace and harmony. We got to listen to each other's point of view in a loving and peaceful way, which fostered an environment of growth and learning. We shared many tears as we sympathized with each other's pain. We greatly respect each other and treasure the wonderful memories, especially the unforgettable laughs we shared in France, and later back in California.

It is very tragic for me today to see how hatred hardens most peoples' hearts and often kills their conscience. It leaves no room for dialogue or understanding. It is blinding. It saddens me to see over and over how people from different cultures, religions, countries, ethnicities, or even skin colors tend to focus on what divides and separates them from others, instead of finding the common ground that unites them. I perceive it as a struggle of pride or ego. Due to a spirit of self-righteousness and lack of humility, each side continuously tries to prove their correctness and the others' fallacy. Consequently, any efforts to reach peace and harmony are engulfed with lies, misinterpretations and propaganda while usually being fueled by hatred and ignorance. People die or murder others over this madness. The true God who is *love* is completely absent in all these scenarios even if His name gets deceptively used. I identify this as pure evil, regardless of who does it or under what banner it is done. Divisions caused by self-righteousness and destruction of life are never from God. I have lived and experienced many cultures, countries and religions. The majority of human beings on earth are seeking the same things from life. We want to love and be loved. We want to live with dignity, to be respected, to have our basic needs met in life, to be productive and to live in peace, without fear.

Overall, I was learning a lot about France but mostly I was learning about myself. I matured significantly as weeks went by and I felt stronger about my values and beliefs as they were frequently put to the test. There were many temptations and the truth is I could have done anything I wanted and nobody would have ever found out about it. I am happy to say that I passed my *own* rigorous standards and came out strengthened by the experience.

In November 1989, an unexpected news report grabbed my full attention while watching television. The reporter talked about the historic collapse of the Berlin Wall that divided Eastern and Western Germany. The reporter continued to talk about signs indicating the beginning of the collapse of the Soviet Union and communism in general.

Suddenly, my heart started beating really fast and my mind started racing. A sudden memory flashed through my mind that took me back to the year 1985. The word "Medjugorje" popped in my mind in big bolded fluorescent colors. Most likely you are wondering *"What is that?"* Let me try to explain, so please bear with me as I briefly take you back in time. Hopefully, I will not confuse you too much.

While I was in high school in 1985, my parents received a tape cassette from an Egyptian man who ate at their restaurant. This was years before CDs, MP3s or DVDs were invented. The man taped his story after his visit to a small mountain village called "Medjugorje" (pronounced as Med-jee-gorya) which was located, at that time, in the southeast European communist country of Yugoslavia. (In 1991, the former country of Yugoslavia broke apart into several independent countries. Medjugorje is now located in the country of Bosnia-Herzegovina.)[8] This is a village where the mother of the Lord Jesus Christ, commonly known as the "Blessed Virgin Mary," has been appearing daily since June 24, 1981 to six Croatian children. She identified herself to them as the "Blessed Virgin Mary, Queen of Peace." She continues to appear daily to three of the six children, who are called the "visionaries" because they were able to see her physically when she appeared to them. They speak to her exactly in the same manner as they speak to any human being. She has conveyed many messages to the world through them.

Just to clarify, as of the year 2007, these visionaries are no longer children. They are now adults who are in their mid-thirties to early forties. The Blessed Virgin Mary told them that she was sent to earth with God's permission, with the mission of promoting peace between God and mankind, through her Son, Jesus. She told them that she came to tell the world that God exists. God *is* the fullness of life, and to enjoy this fullness and peace, humans must return to God.

The Egyptian man, who brought the cassette to my parents, had a daughter who was dying of cancer. He took her to the village of Medjugorje and she was miraculously healed. Therefore, this man made a promise to God to tape his story and circulate it in thanksgiving for his daughter's healing. I do not know why, but even at the age of fifteen, I felt a strong urge

---

[8] For further information about Medjugorje, please visit the official website of Medjugorje at www.medjugorje.hr or at another thorough website on Medjugorje at www.medjugorje.org

in my heart to pay attention. So I took the tape from my parents and quietly listened to it in my room.

As I carefully listened, I became amazed by his story. I have, and have always had a special place in my heart for the Blessed Virgin Mary. Even as a child, I considered her to be my heavenly mother; therefore I listened to the tape with great interest. This man said one thing that stuck in my mind the most. He said that the Blessed Virgin Mary promised that through prayer, Russia would be converted and communism would collapse. It was 1985 and this seemed too far-fetched for me. If you are old enough to remember, we were in the middle of the Cold War and there was no such thing as Russia at the time. The country was referred to as the Soviet Union.

So, during the year of study in France,1989-1990, the events in the world started unfolding; communism was indeed collapsing very fast which led to the fall of the Berlin Wall and was followed by the collapse of the Soviet Union. The world of communism, that many of us feared, seemed to be coming to an end. The word "Russia" suddenly resurfaced in the media. All these events triggered my memory of the tape I had previously heard.

The news impacted me in such a profound way. For some reason, suddenly, I had a burning desire in my heart to go to Medjugorje. I could not stop thinking about it. In fact, you could even say it became an obsession. I could not explain it as this feeling was very foreign to me. I wanted to go and "check it out" for myself. I was living too close not to take advantage. I felt compelled to write to Andrea in Spain and suggest a slight change in plans. As I previously mentioned, Andrea was agnostic then so she did not want to hear anything related to God or religion. I was afraid that she would not approve a short stop in Medjugorje.

I later visited Andrea in Spain and was able to strike a deal with her. I told her that if she would allow a small detour during our pre-planned trip and come with me to Medjugorje for two days, I would go to any country she wanted to add to the itinerary. Andrea wanted to go to Hungary so we agreed to add it to our trip and also make a short stop in Medjugorje on our train ride from Italy to Greece. Geographically, the train had to go through the country of Yugoslavia to arrive to Greece.

I could never imagine what was awaiting me next!

Chapter Five

Planting the Seeds in Medjugorje

"For God so loved the world that he gave his only Son, so that everyone who believes in him might not perish but might have eternal life. For God did not send his Son into the world to condemn the world, but that the world might be saved through him."

- John 3: 16-18

In June 1990, we completed our academic year in Europe. I traveled by train, along with Andrea and another friend, Betsy, whom I had met in my program in France and we began eagerly exploring Europe. After we toured the cities of Milan and Venice in northern Italy, we headed to Yugoslavia. We took the train to a city called Mostar. We then took a public bus for a short ride to Medjugorje. The three of us were going there with absolutely no expectations. We were curious, but we did not know that much about this place. We planned to stay there one night and depart the following day to head south to Greece. I had no idea why I was going to Medjugorje. I knew in my heart that something beyond my understanding was pulling me to this place. I had to see it myself to satisfy this strong urge within me.

From the moment I stepped off the bus in Medjugorje, I felt a tremendous sense of peace that I had never experienced before. Andrea and

Betsy shared these feelings of peace and contentment, which grew in me by the hour. It was a small village, bustling with pilgrims from all over the world. The first thing that we noticed was a big white church, called St. James Church, with two white towers on each side. Behind the church, we saw a mountain crowned by an enormous white cement cross. We had no idea why the cross was up there and we assumed that they built it to commemorate the place where the Virgin Mary first appeared. We later found out that it was called Mount Krizevac or the "Cross Mountain."

We did not have any reservations anywhere and most places were already booked. We noticed that there were many long benches outside of the church and decided to spend the night sleeping on them, believing we could use the church's bathrooms to freshen up the next morning.

Around 6 P.M. that evening, thousands of people gathered in and around the church, praying the rosary. This is a Catholic prayer that meditates on the life and various events of Jesus' life, taken directly from the New Testament of the Bible. They are called the Mysteries of the Rosary and are divided into four main parts. The Joyful Mysteries contemplate the first twelve years of Jesus' life. The Luminous Mysteries contemplate His three years of ministry as He fulfilled His mission on earth. The Sorrowful Mysteries contemplate His agony, passion, crucifixion and death. Finally the Glorious Mysteries contemplate His resurrection and ascension into heaven. It is prayed on what is called "rosary beads." Although I was raised Catholic, and recalled seeing my grandmother praying the rosary in Jordan when I was a child, I did not know how to pray this prayer. I only knew how to pray the prayers that are repeated during the contemplation of the mysteries, such as the "Our Father" and "Hail Mary" prayers.

What impressed me the most was seeing hundreds of men, women, teenagers and children kneeling down and praying inside and outside of the church. I could hear many different languages reciting the prayers together. I felt such a reverence and stillness in the air. After the rosary was over at 7 P.M., the evening Mass was started. Looking toward the altar, I saw an uplifting sight that I had never seen before. There, instead of only one priest, stood over 30 priests from all over the world, concelebrating the service together. I had never attended a Mass service so multi-lingual, but yet so harmonized. I heard the Gospel reading repeated in about six or eight languages.

After Mass was over, we were told it was possible to go up the Cross Mountain. We decided to climb up to see if there was anything unusual about it. We headed toward the mountain around 8:30 P.M. I was surprised that they did not have anything similar to a ski lift to get us to the top.

As we started hiking the rocky path, we realized that the climb to the top was meant to be a spiritual pilgrimage or experience. The mountain was adorned by what was called the "Stations of the Cross." These were a series of 14 bronze sculptures depicting the main scenes of Jesus Christ's sufferings and death. As we climbed up, the sun was quickly setting and we realized we had no flashlights. We decided to just cautiously ascend until we finally reached the top around 10:00 P.M. that evening. The cross was much bigger than we had perceived from below.

We were approached by an elderly woman who asked us in English why we were there that night and not on Apparition Hill. We did not understand what she was talking about. She explained to us that the Virgin Mary was going to have an apparition that evening with some of the visionaries at 11

P.M. on Apparition Hill. This was the hill where the children first saw her in 1981 and she had appeared many times to them at that location. We responded that we thought this mountain was the apparition place since there was a huge cross on top of it.

She proceeded to explain that the fifteen-ton concrete cross was constructed in 1933 by the villagers in thanksgiving for the cessation of crop damaging hail storms and to commemorate the 1900 years since the death and resurrection of Jesus. It took much hard labor and the dedication of the entire village to build the cross. They carried by hand, up the 1770 foot mountain, all the material which went into its construction. The building of the cross gave us a clue as to why the Virgin Mary chose this region for the manifestation of her love and concern for her children on earth. The woman then suggested showing us the way to Apparition Hill. She told us that if we rushed down the mountain with her, we might arrive in time for the apparition.

We looked at each other and started sprinting down the mountain. We knew that this was something very unusual and wanted to experience it. To this day, I do not understand how we were able to race down that rocky mountain with no flashlights and without getting hurt. It took us less than an hour to get down. We ran the whole way trying to keep up with the elderly woman. We were amazed by her strength despite her age. When we got to Apparition Hill, we were crushed to see a crowd of pilgrims coming down the hill with their flashlights. We knew we had missed the apparition. We were extremely disappointed, but decided to wait for all the pilgrims to come down so that we could go up to check out the hill. Thankfully, this hill was much smaller than the Cross Mountain and we were able to reach the top within ten minutes.

We saw a normal size cross that was placed in the area where the visionaries first saw the Virgin Mary. Betsy and Andrea decided to look around while I took a few minutes to go down on my knees and pray. While I was in prayer, I heard Andrea eagerly calling to get our attention. She told us that she could not believe how far we ran to get to the hill we were on. I could not understand what she was saying as it was 11:30 P.M. and the night was very dark, so how could she tell how far we had come? I could not see any of the mountains around that we saw visible during the day. She pointed, telling us to look at the big red cross on top of Cross Mountain. Betsy and I both looked over and saw the cross illuminated in a flaming red color. That was the only thing visible in the entire mountain chain around us. We did not think too much about this sight, but discussed the distance and the speed of our journey to Apparition Hill. We headed back to the church's outdoor benches to get some sleep.

The next morning, we got up early as there were people going into the church for the early Croatian Mass. Just to clarify, starting at 8 am every day of the year, there are at least five Mass services held daily in that church for the pilgrims who are visiting from all over the world. The Masses are held in many languages, including, but not limited to, English, German, Italian, French, Croatian and sometimes Spanish.

We knew there was an English Mass at 10 am so we decided to attend the service since our bus was not leaving until noon. After Mass, we sat on a bench outside the church eating our lunch and getting ready for our departure. Unexpectedly, a woman approached us and asked if she could join the three of us on the bench. We welcomed her as she sat down next to Andrea across from me and Betsy. She told us that she was from Australia and asked us if we had attended the apparition that occurred the night before on Apparition Hill. We explained to her what transpired and how we arrived too late. She said she had been there. We eagerly asked her to tell us what happened and if she had been able to see the Virgin Mary.

This Australian woman explained that she did not see anything with her eyes. Only the visionaries were able to see the Virgin Mary when she appeared. She stated that all the pilgrims were in prayer together awaiting the apparition but when the Virgin Mary finally appeared, everyone quieted down and there was a deep silence. The Australian woman could see the visionaries looking at something and speaking to someone. The woman was able to feel a "presence" although she could not see anything.

She then added a detail that got our full attention. She said that after the apparition ended, there was something miraculous that happened and not many pilgrims noticed. When people were heading down the hill, she looked over to Cross Mountain and saw the cross flaming red. We looked at her a bit puzzled and did not understand why she called that "miraculous." We had seen this too, but assumed that the cross was electrically illuminated during the night. The woman explained that there was no electricity at all around the cross, within the cross, or anywhere on the mountain. It was physically impossible for the cross to light up or be seen at night.

The three of us looked at each other in disbelief. Andrea looked like she had seen a ghost. After all, she was the one who first noticed the cross and pointed it out to me and Betsy. We did not believe what the woman was telling us. We thought that she was either exaggerating things or that she did not know what she was talking about. There had to be electric power in that cross. We knew what our eyes saw. In fact, as I write this paragraph, I can still close my eyes and envision what I saw that night, although this occurred over seventeen years ago. I saw a huge flaming red cross. I could even see the width, the height and the depth of it. It was fully illuminated.

The three of us did not know what to do about what we had just heard. Our bus was supposed to leave within that hour. We needed to make a fast decision. I looked at Andrea to see what she was thinking. We both knew that we could not leave like this. We needed to investigate the cross for ourselves, in daylight this time. The three of us decided to postpone our departure until the following day. The Australian woman then proceeded to tell each of us very personal things about our pasts and in my case, prophetic things about my future. We did not know how she knew things about our lives. She then gave us each the name of a different saint. She said we should learn about that saint's life as it would provide us powerful lessons for our own lives. For me, she gave me the name of Saint Anthony. At the time, I had never heard of this saint. I believe she was referring to the saint commonly known as St. Anthony of Padua. He is known for his intercession in helping to find lost objects and to obtain a miracle. He spent his whole life learning how to be closer to God, and, how to love God more deeply. He became very famous for his preaching and evangelizing because he spoke passionately and forcefully.

We started heading up the mountain at noon and this time we were on an investigative mission. When we finally made it to the base of the gigantic cross, we proceeded to circle around it, looking for an electric plug or some power source. To our complete amazement, we could find none. The cross was pure cement. Something was happening to the three of us. We did not know who this Australian woman was, but her message to us changed the course of the remainder of our trip. As far as I am concerned, she was instrumental in my life's mission. Over the years, I often wondered to myself who the Australian and the elderly ladies truly were. Were they really human or were they angels sent to us by God to deliver important messages? We never saw them again.

When we came down from the mountain, we met some friendly British men who told us that Medjugorje had changed their lives. One of them had been living there for several months. He had previously been involved with the occult and satanic practices and had had no interest in God. He came to Medjugorje only because of a promise that he had made to his very ill mother. In Medjugorje he was able to experience God's love and mercy for the first time in his life. His heart was changed and he committed his life to serving Jesus Christ.

We told them what we had experienced the night before. They confirmed that the cross was usually not visible at night. They suggested to us that what occurred was a sign for the three of us, that it was not an accident that the Australian woman approached us one hour before our intended departure, and that we were meant to stay in Medjugorje for a reason. These men added that we happened to be there during the week of the nine year anniversary of the apparitions. The apparitions began on June 24, 1981 when the visionaries first saw the Blessed Virgin Mary on the hill. She did not speak to them that day as they were scared and ran away. The following day, they felt an urge to return and that was when she first spoke to them. That is why the actual anniversary is celebrated each year on the 25th of June.

We had arrived in Medjugorje around June 20, 1990. Many pilgrims purposefully flew there during that week for the anniversary. Our new British friends told us that we ought to stay the week and see what our Lord Jesus had in store for us, as our trip seemed to be divinely planned.

We agreed to extend our stay. Our new friends helped us find lodging in one of the boarding homes - they did not have any motels or hotels in the village at the time. None of us could deny that something was happening that surpassed our intellectual understanding. We anxiously awaited the arrival of the night to see if the cross would light up again after dark. We sat there outside the church facing the mountain. As the night grew darker, we were unable to see Cross Mountain. The cross was not visible at all. In fact, we were never able to see it again at night. The weather was very clear during the summer nights; however, the mountains were dark with the moon as their only source of light.

During the course of that week, we talked to many people and heard many conversion stories. We attended the daily Mass services and participated in the events that were happening in the church. For the first time in my life, I was not monitoring my watch during the Mass service. I did not care if the priest's homily was long. I was thirsty to hear the word of God. We were in prayer services for three to four hours every evening and I was not bored. In fact, I started feeling this incredible joy that I had never experienced before. Something was happening within my heart that I could not mentally understand.

I remember one evening, while praying inside the church - during adoration of our Lord Jesus through His Presence in the exposed Blessed Sacrament - I experienced an incredible feeling of love that completely overwhelmed me. It was as if God's love engulfed me. I started sobbing and cried for a couple of hours. As I knelt down, I allowed my head to drop to the floor as I wept and wept, forming a small puddle of water all around me. My weeping was not caused by any sadness. It was an emotion that was foreign to me. I felt this intense heat within my heart and the rest of my body, feeling extremely loved like never before. God's love was cleansing and purifying me from the inside out as His immense love melted my heart. At that moment, I knew beyond a shadow of a doubt that God existed and was real. Although born and raised Christian, I never had a personal relationship with Jesus. That night, I felt Jesus so deeply in my heart that I knew, for the first time in my life, the extent of His love for me. I knew that He died for *me* personally, just like He did for everyone else, including *you*, regardless of your religion or background. That evening I experienced a glimpse of what would await us in heaven. I had tasted a piece of heaven while still on earth. This was the first time in my life that I was not afraid to die.

For the first time since I was eight years old, I went to confession. Just to explain briefly, through sacred scripture and the traditions and teachings of the Catholic Church, Catholics believe that the Lord Jesus, through a priest, hears our sins and pardons us.[9] "Sin" is our failure or refusal to live the life that God intends for us; it is an act of failure or refusal to obey God's

---

[9] John 20:22-23

commandments.[10] Even though the priest is also a sinner and just a human being, the Lord uses him as an instrument to channel His love and mercy. It is actually a very humbling experience for me to go and confess my sins before another human being, regardless of how sinful or holy the other person is. Pride has been my enemy over the years so I welcome all experiences that assist me in ridding myself of it. Of course, I am still working on that!

There were over ten priests, from all over the world, listening to confessions in different languages. I joined the pilgrims who waited patiently for hours in the long lines to go to confession. This was something I had never experienced before. Back in the United States, confessions were usually held for one hour before Mass, once a week. Since few people confessed their sins, one priest was usually sufficient to meet the low demand.

When I finally arrived in the confessional, I knelt face to face before the priest who was an elderly Irish man. I stayed there for almost an hour and wept the whole time. This was another occasion when I felt Jesus' incredible love and mercy overwhelm me. The priest's voice was filled with compassion and gentleness as he counseled me. He looked at me and told me gently: *"Don't you know how much Jesus loves you? Don't you know He died for you on the cross? Go in His peace and enjoy His love for you."*

---

[10] The Catechism of the Catholic Church defines "sin" as: "an offense against God as well as fault against reason, truth and right conscience. Sin is a deliberate thought, word, deed, or omission contrary to the eternal law or God." (1849, 1853, 1854).

I left the confessional booth feeling like a new person, so much lighter, as if a heavy weight was released from my back. It looked brighter outside. I felt so clean from within, so rejuvenated and so grateful to be alive.

On the following afternoon, I was standing with Andrea and Betsy outside of St. James Church. It was around 5:30 P.M. The sun was still hot and bright. Suddenly, we heard some people screaming next to us, telling everyone to look quickly at the sun. I turned around to see what they were looking at. I was completely astounded by the miraculous view we witnessed. Without any difficulty, I was able to look straight at the sun, without sunglasses. It was spinning rapidly around its own axis. Then suddenly, it started pulsating from right to left and also forward toward us. The sun was dancing and projecting or emanating many beautiful colors. At that moment, many people were standing outside the church, maybe around fifty or sixty people. We were all witnessing the same event and people shouted out what they were seeing. It was one of the most beautiful sights I had ever seen in my life. As it quickly dawned on me that we were once again witnessing another miraculous event, I fell to the ground and started weeping feeling so small and so humbled by God's infinite power. The enormous sun suddenly appeared like a tiny child's yo-yo toy in God's hands. I could not help but wonder if my faith was still so weak that God had to show me another sign to believe. We later found out that this frequent phenomenon was called "the miracle of the dancing sun." Thousand of pilgrims have witnessed the sun dance over the years, though not everyone who has gone to Medjugorje has witnessed it.

As the week progressed, we learned more about the Medjugorje apparitions, and we were able to be present during a public apparition. The

Apparition Hill was packed with pilgrims. I could not see the visionaries while the apparition was happening; however, I felt a very strong supernatural presence and peace during those moments. We understood why the Blessed Virgin Mary had been appearing daily for many years. In a nutshell, she had been appearing in accordance with God's directives to call people throughout the world back to her son Jesus Christ. She called herself the "Blessed Virgin Mary, Queen of Peace." As His mother, she personally experienced His immense love for everyone as she watched Him lay down His life for all of God's children. She taught the visionaries that in order for human beings to have peace in the world, humans must first reconcile with God and have peace in their individual hearts and also in their families. She was calling humanity to conversion and to change its way of life.

One important thing that the Blessed Virgin Mary emphasized was that the devil, Satan, is real and not an imaginary character. The devil's biggest triumph in the past century has been his ability to convince the world that he does not exist. Most people have stopped believing he is real; consequently, he has been able to accomplish much destruction and evil in the world. The Blessed Virgin Mary is reminding everyone that just as God is very real so is His enemy, the devil. Although the Lord Jesus triumphed over Satan through His death and resurrection, Satan's reign in this world has not yet ended. He is more active now than ever before and is attempting to destroy the souls of God's children.

The Blessed Virgin Mary is urgently calling us to prayer, especially prayer with the heart. She urges us to pray to God out of love and not out of obligation. Prayer is how we connect to God. As we were created by Him, we need to be connected to Him through prayer to have inner peace and His guidance in our lives. She is calling us to pray the rosary. Since the rosary is a synopsis of the Gospel and a meditation on Jesus' life, it is a powerful tool against the devil and he cannot tolerate this prayer. She is asking us to fast on bread and water on Wednesdays and Fridays as fasting strengthens the soul and the willpower, to read the Holy Bible everyday, to attend Mass more frequently - daily if possible, and to confess our sins at least monthly to keep our souls clean and receptive to God.

Just to clarify, this was not the first time in human history that the Blessed Virgin Mary has appeared to people who were able to see her with their human eyes. There are many well-known apparition sites that have been approved by the Catholic Church, such as the apparitions of Fatima in Portugal, of Guadalupe in Mexico City, of Lourdes in France, of Zeitun in Egypt and many other places. Since the apparitions of Medjugorje have been going on since 1981, the Catholic Church has not yet issued a decision approving or denying them. In accordance with Church procedure in such cases, the authenticity of these apparitions does not come to a final determination until after the apparitions come to an end. The church has to investigate the legitimacy of these apparitions and ensure that the visionaries are truthful and not seeing demonic spirits. The Blessed Virgin Mary in Medjugorje told the visionaries that after the apparitions were completed, God would leave a visible, permanent, great sign on Apparition Hill to authenticate the apparitions. We do not know yet the exact date when this will occur; however, the sign will be irrefutable and will serve as a proof of her apparitions. It will be something that has never been on the earth before.

After our week was over, we continued with our original plans and departed to Greece. I remember the long train ride as we headed south. I was very contemplative and feeling very changed. Although I witnessed the miracle of the cross flaming red and the miracle of the dancing sun, the most important and greatest miracle that had happened there was the conversion that occurred in my heart. Miracles are meaningless if they do not transform our hearts. In Medjugorje, I felt like a veil had lifted from my eyes, as if I was given a glimpse of the spiritual world and the heavenly realm. I finally discovered the spiritual eyes of my heart. I knew my life would never be the same.

Chapter Six

Change in Travel Plans

"But seek first the kingdom [of God] and his righteousness, and all these things will be given you besides. Do not worry about tomorrow; tomorrow will take care of itself."

- Mathew 6: 33-34

W e took the train through Athens and then headed directly to the Island of Crete. It was beautiful there. I tried to enjoy the delightful scenery around me, however, something within me was so transformed, that I had no more desire to travel in Europe. Despite the beauty of Greece, nothing was fulfilling to me anymore. It was as if I tasted a piece of heaven and was struggling to go back to earth. I had about three weeks left of my trip in Europe and my heart was yearning to go back to Medjugorje. I tried to disconnect the desire but found it impossible. I started experiencing the emptiness of the material world around me. You see, despite the simplicity of the village of Medjugorje, I felt complete there. It was a very basic lifestyle, surrounded with farms and modest people. What was striking about these villagers was their faith. They truly lived their faith and it showed through the love they emanated.

I did not know what to do. Although I had dreamt about visiting Greece ever since I was a child, my heart felt anxious there. I did not know how to tell Andrea and Betsy that I no longer wanted to continue my tour of Europe. I had no desire to see anything else after Medjugorje. Everything else seemed so superficial and empty in comparison to the depth of spirituality that I had experienced. I felt a strong pull to return to Medjugorje for the remaining time we had left.

I finally broke the news to them. Although Andrea was disappointed, she was not surprised. She told me that she understood my decision. She agreed that something was happening there; however, she could not accompany me. She needed to take time to decipher the events she had experienced in Medjugorje as they had challenged her own belief system. We decided to separate in Yugoslavia as we traveled back north through that country. Betsy decided at the last minute to return to Medjugorje with me instead of continuing her trip with Andrea. In case you are wondering if Andrea is still agnostic, she recently informed me that she *does* believe in God now and has believed in Him for a long time.[11]

When we arrived again in Medjugorje, my heart felt at home again. I was extremely happy. I had a couple of weeks to spend there so I decided to try to live according to what Mary was asking of us, prayerful life, fasting, daily Mass, confession and reading the Bible. Despite my love for food, the Lord gave me the grace (God's gratuitous divine assistance) to fast on bread and water the entire time I was there. My trip this time was a true pilgrimage. I spent countless hours in prayer, like never before.

Just as our Lord was revealing to me His love and mercy, He also allowed me to endure a difficult incident to expose to me the face of evil in the world. The Lord also showed me the power of His protective love. What

---

[11] Neither Betsy nor Andrea ever returned to Medjugorje since 1990.

I will be sharing with you next is very difficult for me to convey, as it is very delicate. In the past few years, I have received a lot of inner-healing around this incident. I have never previously related this incident to my own family and was not planning on including it in this chapter. After much prayer and resistance on my part, the Lord has guided me to share the experience and include it in these words.

When Betsy and I returned to Medjugorje, we were extremely enthusiastic about our new relationship with our Lord. Therefore, we decided to spend two entire nights in prayer on Apparition Hill and then on the top of Cross Mountain. However, the second night that we spent on Cross Mountain was extremely cold, and I did not have a jacket or a blanket to keep me warm. As a result, I got terribly sick and feverish that night. Amazingly, a huge stray dog suddenly appeared out of nowhere and snuggled next to me keeping me warm as he blocked off the cold winds. The following morning when we descended from the mountain, I could barely walk. We ran into a man we had previously met on our first trip who owned one of the boarding houses by the bus stop. Although he was a young man in his twenties and appeared handsome and friendly, there was just something about him that my heart could not trust. He saw how sick I was and informed us that he had some vacant rooms in his boarding house. We agreed to stay there, as I was very weak from my fever. I needed to lie down as I had not slept in two days.

I rested well that night, however, when I woke up the following morning, I still felt physically very weak. Betsy decided to go to the morning English Mass alone so she left the room while I stayed in bed. About ten minutes later, I heard the key turning in the doorknob so I assumed that Betsy had forgotten something. To my complete shock, the owner of the boarding house entered into the room with his own master key. He had seen Betsy leaving for Mass and knew that I was left in the room alone. As he quickly approached the bed, my heart sunk deeply within me as I dreaded the worst. I asked him in English what he wanted or what he was doing there. He did not respond and proceeded to climb up on the bed where I was lying lifelessly. Looking into his eyes, I could see much evil flaring outward toward me. The face of the devil emerged from what previously had appeared as a young and friendly man. My mind was racing extremely fast, as I could not absorb what was transpiring. I was twenty years old at the time, an innocent virgin, lying down feverishly on a bed in the holy village of Medjugorje during a spiritual pilgrimage. Yet, the devil was busily lurking through this man to vandalize my encounter with God and deprive me of my *innocence* and purity in the moment I least expected it. Furthermore, as you recall, I grew up with such shaming attached to the loss of virginity; rape was the worst thing that anyone could do to me.

My mind was imagining the worst as this man straddled me on the bed while immobilizing my arms with his legs. At that moment, I completely froze and lost my ability to scream or shout. In fact, I felt like my spirit disconnected and left my body. As strange and unbelievable as this might sound to you, I saw myself floating on top of the bed and looking at the scene below me with this man on top of me beginning to unzip his pants to expose himself. All I could see were tears running down my motionless cheeks. Suddenly, in complete faith, my soul screamed so loud to our Heavenly Father with an inaudible inner voice saying:

"FATHER!!!! You cannot allow this to happen to me! If my earthly father were here, he would probably kill this man. You are my Heavenly

Father and you are everywhere and all-powerful. You have to do something to stop this NOW even if you have to shake the earth."

As soon as my heart finished shouting these pleading words and without any physical movement on my part, I suddenly saw this man jolted backwards off of me and almost falling off the bed. He saw me completely motionless but yet some incredible, invisible force had pushed him off the bed before he could cause me any more harm. He looked extremely startled and frightened as he staggered backwards and dashed out of the room. And me? I know beyond a shadow of a doubt that our Heavenly Father had heard my resounding prayer and had protected me instantaneously with his powerful angels.

After he left, I weakly got out of bed and packed all of my belongings. I knew I needed to leave that place right away. I somehow packed Betsy's luggage and left the room. Fortunately I was able to locate her after Mass and informed her of what had transpired. We were able to find another vacant boarding house at the side of the church and I tried to place this horrible incident behind me. It was clear to me that the Lord allowed me to know that the devil was real and actively working everywhere, including holy places. It is precisely when people are trying to get closer to God that the devil feels the most threatened. He was working through this man, who physically appeared attractive, trying to allure me, just like many material things in the world try to entice us. I felt very thankful and blessed that the Lord saved me from what could have been a life-long traumatic experience.

Although I was not raped or physically hurt, I was still emotionally scarred and wounded by this incident. My wounds created a hole in my heart that the devil filled with shame, guilt and even self-blame but our Lord Jesus has never failed to amaze me with His generous and merciful love which heals even the deepest wounds of the heart. As you will read in later chapters, through the inner-healing work that I later experienced, Jesus healed, and is continuously healing, many of my heart's wounds.

As the days went by, I felt like I was truly in heaven and did not want to leave. There was something very profound happening in my heart. I felt a tremendous call by God to do something. It felt like a strong prompting, or inner urge to give my life to God. He was asking me for me "yes." I could not understand the exact nature of God's call. I remember one day just weeping and offering my life and my will to God. Although from a young age I had aspired to become a lawyer to help and serve people, I told our Lord that I was willing to become a nun if that was what He was asking of me; however, He needed to give me a clear sign. I was willing to do whatever He was asking. At that time, I thought that the only way God called us to serve Him was through religious life. Of course I know now that we can serve God in many different ways; it just took me many years to learn that.

Incidentally, I remember one day calling my parents in California and telling them that I planned to stay in Medjugorje and that I did not want to go back to the United States. Understandably, my worried mother told me in a concerned voice that I needed to come back and finish my university education first and then we would revisit the issue. I think they believed I had lost my mind.

My life was eternally changed by my trip to Medjugorje. The visionaries said that the Blessed Virgin Mary told them that nobody went there by accident, or mere coincidence. Everyone went there for a reason and by invitation. This was very true for me. I was invited to open myself to God in ways I had never done before. The seeds of His love were deeply planted in my heart. I learned so much about Jesus and His immense love for me and you in Medjugorje. Although I grew up Catholic and went to the Mass service weekly, I had never completely understood or appreciated the greatness of what actually transpired there. An actual miracle occurs every time Mass or Liturgical services are being celebrated. During Mass, Catholics receive the "Eucharist" which is also known as the "Blessed Sacrament." Actually the word "Eucharist" comes from the Greek word *"eucharistia"* which means "thanksgiving." It is a Sacrament that was instituted by Jesus during the Last Supper, as recorded in the Gospels of Matthew, Mark and Luke.[12] Through sacred scripture and the traditions and teachings of the Catholic Church, Catholics believe that the bread and wine consecrated by the priest during Mass become the true Body, Blood, Soul and Divinity of the Lord Jesus Christ. This process is called "transubstantiation," although the appearance of the bread and wine is not altered. As Jesus told us through His apostle John: *"Amen, amen, I say to you, unless you eat the flesh of the Son of Man and drink his blood, you do not have life within you. Whoever eats my flesh and drinks my blood has eternal life, and I will raise him on the last day. For my flesh is true food, and my blood is true drink."*[13]

The Catholic faith teaches that Jesus literally meant His words and was not speaking symbolically, as He repeated the same words various times throughout Chapter Six of the Gospel of John. In fact, Jesus was so literal that many of His disciples left Him and went back to their former way of life

---

[12] Mathew 26: 26-28, Mark 14: 22-24, Luke 22: 17-20
[13] John 6: 53-58; see also 1Corinthians 11:23-29

as it was too hard for them to accept His teaching.[14] That is precisely why the Blessed Virgin Mary is calling people to try to go to daily Mass to be able to receive her Son Jesus, through receiving the Eucharist. I often heard that Satanists believed Jesus was really present in the Blessed Sacrament. They often paid people to steal the consecrated Host from Catholic churches during communion. They desecrated and violated the Host in the most atrocious ways because they believed they were torturing Jesus.

The Blessed Virgin Mary is also calling people to spend time with Him through His Presence in the Blessed Sacrament. This is what Roman Catholics refer to as "Adoration of the Blessed Sacrament." She emphasizes that to know Him, we need to spend intimate time with Him, in silent prayer, so that He can talk to us and transform and heal our hearts.

Many people misunderstand Catholics because of their devotion to, and love for, Mary. I have been previously accused of worshipping Mary because I pray for her intercessions. Nothing is further away from the truth. Catholics worship *only* God. Mary was human and not a "god" to be worshipped. To me, Mary *is* my heavenly mother, just like I believe she is everyone else's mother, regardless of their religious background, creed or beliefs. She is the one who, initially through my Medjugorje experience, took me to Jesus and taught me about Him. As His mother, she knew Him the best. She pointed me only to Him, never to herself, and showed me the way to love Him and receive His love. Mary was an incredibly humble and loving woman. She was chosen by God from all the women throughout history to be the mother of His Son Jesus. Through her obedience and willingness, Jesus was conceived by the Holy Spirit and born into humanity. Jesus gave Mary to all

---

[14] John 6:60 and John 6:66

65

of us as our spiritual mother while He was dying on the cross. He told Mary to behold her son John, referring to his apostle who was standing next to her. Jesus then turned to John and told him to behold his mother.[15] As John was the only apostle present at the crucifixion, John represented the church, making Mary our mother. Ever since then, Mary has been faithful throughout history, caring for all of her children around the world. As a matter of fact, my personal favorite way of referring to her is by calling her "mommy Mary." This allows me to feel more intimately connected to her. Throughout my life, she has proven to me, time after time, that she is truly my spiritual mother.

As I look back now, I know beyond a shadow of a doubt, that the main reason for me to have studied in France was so that I could go to Medjugorje. Of course, none of this was planned by me. Only God could orchestrate something as incredible as this. He also knew that my parents would never consent for me to travel to Europe or go to Medjugorje alone. God had this planned even when I was still living in Jordan. As I mentioned in my second chapter, my parents happened to place me and my brothers in the best school for teaching French in the whole country. I do not believe there are any coincidences or accidents in life. Everything serves its purpose in due time. As of today, nobody in my family has ever gone to Medjugorje. The invitation from God, through The Blessed Virgin Mary, was for me alone. He did not force me, but only prompted my heart. I accepted the invitation and thus my life had been changed permanently.

---

[15] John 19: 26-27

Chapter Seven

Returning to the United States

"...God has exhibited us apostles as the last of all, like people sentenced to death, since we have become a spectacle to the world, to angels and human beings alike. We are fools on Christ's account, but you are wise in Christ; we are weak, but you are strong; you are held in honor, but we in disrespect. To this very hour we go hungry and thirsty, we are poorly clad and roughly treated, we wander about homeless and we toil, working with our own hands. When ridiculed, we bless; when persecuted, we endure; when slandered, we respond gently. We have become like the world's rubbish, the scum of all, to this very moment."

- 1 Corinthians 4: 9-13

After one year of being away from home, I returned to the United States at the end of July 1990. I was very happy to see my family and friends again. I was still consumed by the events in Medjugorje and all that I had learned and experienced. I wanted to relate to everyone who crossed my path what was happening there. To my complete surprise, nobody wanted to hear about it. I thought I had found an incredible treasure and wanted to share it with everyone. However, people looked at me as if I had lost my mind. Most people thought that I had become a fanatic.

I tried to share my story with my own parents. I was met with skepticism and apprehension. My mother insisted that I had no assurance the Blessed Virgin Mary was the one appearing and suggested it could have been the devil; she did not want me to be deceived. I understood and agreed with my mother's concerns as we must always authenticate any spirits that appear to people. There have been many instances throughout history where the devil appeared as someone else and misguided people. I tried to explain to my mother that if it were truly the devil who was deceiving the visionaries in Medjugorje and appearing disguised as Mary, then he was an incredible fool as thousands of pilgrims, including myself, were converting their lives and turning to God, instead of rejecting Him. I reminded my mother of a teaching from Jesus of how you would know the tree by the fruits it produced. He said: *"...Every good tree bears good fruits, and a rotten tree bears bad fruits. A good tree cannot bear bad fruit, nor can a rotten tree bear good fruit. Every tree that does not bear good fruit will be cut down and thrown into the fire. So by their fruits you will know them."*[16]

I respected my mother's and other people's resistance as not everyone had to agree with my faith or beliefs, including my own family or friends. I love them and ask the Lord to bless their hearts. Ultimately, this is all part of my learning journey on earth, to learn to love unconditionally, to learn to truly forgive with my heart, and to learn to grow spiritually.

As the days went by, I felt extremely lonely and filled with sadness. Nobody was interested in hearing my story. I felt like isolating myself from everyone. At the time, I did not know anyone else who had gone to Medjugorje, besides Andrea and Betsy so I went to the Catholic bookstore

---

[16] Matthew 7: 17-20

and desperately looked for books on Medjugorje. I needed to connect spiritually to someone else who felt the same as I did. To my delight, I found many books by others, not only Catholics, but from different denominations, who had had a huge conversion in Medjugorje. One particular book called *"Medjugorje - The Message"*[17] written by Mr. Wayne Weible, a Lutheran author, helped me tremendously. My soul found much consolation in his book, as I felt understood and accompanied. At least I *knew* that I was not the only one who had had an unusual spiritual experience.

For the following twelve years of my spiritual development and painful growth into maturity, not a day went by that I did not think of Medjugorje, as if I was connected to it by an invisible umbilical cord. As the days went by and the reality of life consumed me, I slowly stopped living the messages of Medjugorje. Sadly, my life sunk back into the "busyness" of the world and after returning with Andrea to California, we rarely discussed my experience.

In September 1990, when I returned to UC Davis to continue my university education, I noticed that the Lord was swiftly gearing me to learn Spanish. Andrea and I shared an apartment for the next two years. Andrea had many friends who came from all over Latin America to work on their graduate level degrees. I became close friends with them as we always ate lunch together. I was invited often to go dancing with them to what is called "Salsa" and "Merengue" music. I was fascinated by how my friends danced with each other to this wonderful Caribbean beat and I resolved to learn. In fact, dancing became my escape from all the university-related pressures and struggles within me. I did not smoke, drink, or take drugs, and I certainly

---

[17] Weible, Wayne. *Medjugorje - The Message.* Paraclete Press, 1989.

could not have a boyfriend but dancing to Salsa and Merengue music became my hobby and my outlet from life's stresses for the following nine years.

The more time I spent with my Latino (Spanish-speaking) friends, the more I realized that it was crucial for me to learn Spanish in order for our friendship to survive. They spoke only Spanish to each other when I was around them, and that became frustrating to me. Although they often translated what they were saying, I knew that I only received the gist of the conversation. They seemed to be having a great time and I wanted to participate in the discussions. They were not trying to be rude or inconsiderate; they were just comfortable speaking in their native tongue.

I decided that it should be easy for me to learn Spanish since it was very similar to French, with the exception of the pronunciation. Spanish was actually much easier to pronounce than French. Thus, during my final year at Davis, I studied one full year of Spanish. I was not scared to speak or make mistakes, so I immersed myself into the rich Latino culture. It was very easy to do that living in California. I started listening only to Spanish radio, watching the Spanish television, particularly Mexican soap-operas, and of course, practicing Spanish with my friends. Before too long, I became fluent in the language.

I am eternally grateful to my Latino friends for all the ways they have blessed and enriched my journey in life. I have learned so much through them about their beautiful cultures and countries that university books could never have taught me. Unbeknownst to them, they were preparing me for an essential part of my spiritual growth that led me to giving my testimony in Spanish to thousands throughout California and in Mexico.

Apart from that, a close friend at UC Davis thought I had a natural gift guiding and counseling people. She saw how many of our friends often trusted me with very intimate and painful details about their lives. She strongly encouraged me to become a peer counselor. I followed her advice and thus volunteered much of my free time working in a confidential peer counseling center called *The House*. It was a free drop-in and phone counseling service where university students could talk to another student about personal and academic problems. Along with all the other student volunteers, I received very structured training and supervision from the licensed therapists and psychologists at UC Davis' Counseling and Psychological Services. We handled many issues ranging from simple roommate or relationship problems, to food disorders, rape, all types of addictions, depression, loneliness, physical abuse, sexual abuse, incest and suicide.

What was so rewarding about this work was how it enabled me to help many students in ways beyond my imagination. In many respects, my conservative upbringing had sheltered me from many horrible things that happen in this world. Of course, I also had my own share of wounds and hurts that caused me much suffering as I explained in my second chapter. Working at *The House* broadened my horizons of the real life issues that other students were dealing with either presently or past, such as rape, physical or sexual abuse and incest. A lot of these issues dealt with wounds that resurfaced from childhood. You see, many students had blocked their childhood trauma as they were unable to deal with the pain or the shame they felt while they were still children, or, while living in the same environment that caused the trauma. Once they moved out on their own, some students had the courage to face their stifling anguish and start the healing process. I was so grateful to be part of the student volunteers' team as the experience was priceless to me. I learned so much. Unbeknownst to me, through this work, the Lord was setting the foundation for my own healing work and the healing work of others that transpired later.

Before leaving this chapter, I feel compelled to mention the unexpected emotional crisis that I endured after returning from Europe at the end of July 1990. As you most likely recall, on August 2, 1990, less than a week after my return, we all became aware of the terrible invasion and occupation of the small country of Kuwait by its giant neighboring country Iraq. Of course, like everyone else, I felt appalled by Iraq's invasion and felt terrible for the Kuwaiti people. After my experience in Medjugorje, I also looked at this event from spiritual eyes and saw the evil that was manifesting itself there between two neighboring Arabic-speaking countries. I prayed daily for a peaceful and quick resolution.

As an Arab-American, the only connection that I had to those events was the same connection other Americans had, with the exception that I was able to speak the Kuwaitis' and Iraqis' Arabic language. As the months went on, it became evident that the United States was preparing to rescue Kuwait, in what became known as the Persian Gulf War, which took place from January 16, 1991 to February 28, 1991.

To my complete astonishment, that period became one of the most painful periods of my life. Although I proudly considered myself an American citizen and I was not at all connected to either Kuwait or Iraq, suddenly Arab-Americans became a target of the blind anti Arab-American hatred that surged in the United States. As you might recall from the news, the hate crimes were alarming. At the time, my parents still owned their small restaurant. I lived daily in fear that someone might walk in and assault or murder them, which was happening to many people who looked Middle Easterner across the United States.

My mind could not comprehend the logic (or lack of it) of what was happening. The United States voluntarily went to liberate Kuwait, an Arabic-speaking country, from Iraq, another Arabic-speaking country. Nevertheless, although I was an American citizen, I became a target of anti Arab-American sentiments, even at UC Davis.

It was the first time since I immigrated to the United States that I thought that my world was crashing down upon me. I started suspecting that my own background and ethnicity might have been cursed. In Jordan, I felt like a second-class citizen since I was considered a "westerner" due to my Christian religion. Suddenly in the U.S., as a result of the tension in the Persian Gulf, I felt like I was singled out again because I was of "Middle Eastern" background, despite my American citizenship.

I fell into a deep depression and despair. I valued many things in the United States, especially the sense of belonging, however, during that period, I felt like I did not belong anywhere. I even contemplated dropping out of the university, as I lost all my enthusiasm for learning in the midst of the ignorance, hatred and insanity that was surrounding me. I endured a very difficult identity crisis for as long as the Gulf War lasted. I was very thankful to God that the war ended after six-weeks. As Kuwait was finally liberated, so was I. Thankfully, I remained in the university and finished my studies.

I graduated from UC Davis in June 1992. I was still thinking frequently about Medjugorje but it started slowly fading away in the back of my mind. I knew in my heart that that path of consecrated religious life was not for me. I decided to take some time off to decide if I still wanted to pursue a legal education. After my volunteer work at *The House,* I saw the wonderful rewards of counseling and started to consider becoming a social worker. I was torn between the two careers and started to pray very hard for the Lord's guidance. Should I apply to law school or should I apply for a Master's degree in Social Work? I asked the Lord for a clear sign.

I moved back to my parents' house right after graduation and lived there for the following two years. Being single and living on my own was not an option in the Middle Eastern culture. Children, or adults, were expected to live with their parents' until they got married, regardless of their age. Since I had been living on my own for the previous five years, moving back with my parents was a challenging and painful experience. I love them dearly; however, it seems that many parents in most cultures never stop seeing their offspring as children, regardless of their age. I am often reminded by my parents that I will understand this when I have children of my own.

After graduation, I tried to obtain employment in counseling centers and non-profit organizations that assisted at-risk youth, but to no avail. I signed up with a temporary employment agency while I was job-hunting. To my surprise, they immediately found me a temporary position as a receptionist working with two lobbyists, who happened to also be lawyers. Even though I did not intend on obtaining this law-related position, it seemed that our Heavenly Father had other plans for me. Looking back, I see His fingerprints engraved on every detail of my life.

I worked there for three months and they offered me a permanent full-time position as a receptionist; however, I knew that after five years of university education, four languages and two bachelor degrees, I was qualified to find something more challenging and productive. So I declined the position and was once again unemployed, thankfully for just that one weekend.

On that Saturday, I happened to go into a coffee shop in Davis where a friend of mine worked. She asked me what I had been doing since graduation. I informed her that I had been working a temporary position that had just ended. To my surprise, my friend told me that one of her regular clients, who had a very advanced position with the California State Department of Education, was looking to employ someone on a full-time basis as an "analyst." This would be a contractual position and not State Civil Service employment (which would have included all the State benefits but would have been a lengthy bureaucratic process for hiring). That woman had just left the coffee shop and gave my friend her private telephone number in case my friend knew of anyone who might be interested. I took the phone number and contacted the woman right away. I interviewed with her on Monday and was employed again on Tuesday, for a contract position that lasted two years, until I headed off to law school in August 1994. As you see, the Lord does really take care of us, if we allow Him to and entrust our lives into His hands. Looking back, this has been true in my life even when it did not seem like it to me at the time.

I thoroughly enjoyed the position, as I learned a lot and was intellectually challenged. I also met some wonderful co-workers who truly cared for the educational system in California, but, I had no health benefits and the pay was low. In addition, due to some legal issues related to the work I was doing, I was exposed, once again, to the lawyers who worked in that

State Department. I felt a strong pull from the Lord to pursue my original desire of becoming a lawyer. It could not have been a pure coincidence that in both jobs after my graduation, I dealt frequently with work of a legal nature.

In the fall of 1993, I started applying to law schools. I prayed a lot during that time and asked God to show me His plan and will for my life. If it was His will for me to go to law school, then I needed to receive at least one letter of acceptance; however, if it was not His will, then I needed to get rejection letters from all the schools, even if that would have killed my ego.

Getting admitted to law school was not as easy as I would have hoped; it was an extremely competitive process. It required excellent grades from the undergraduate university and high scores on the Law School Admission Test (LSAT). To my delight, I got admitted to three private law schools that were all in the San Francisco Bay Area. Although I preferred to go to a public university, such as UC Davis Law School or UCLA, I only received rejection letters from them. Despite the acceptances I did receive, the application process was still a humbling experience. I prayed for guidance; which of these law schools should I attend? They all cost around the same, which, to me, was an extremely large amount of money. I wanted to experience life in San Francisco, so I decided to study at the University of San Francisco, School of Law. I had heard from friends that it was an excellent school. Although I did not have any personal money to finance my education, I was told that it was very easy to obtain student loans for professional schools. I was already carrying some loans from my undergraduate education that I was paying back, but they looked so trivial in comparison to what law school was going to cost me. My parents felt sorry they could not help me out financially. They had a modest income and were making sacrifices to educate my younger sister in a private Catholic elementary school. I felt blessed they were able to do that for my sister, as I knew she needed their help more than I did. I figured that I was an adult and ready to face life on my own.

I was looking at owing around $100,000 by the end of my legal education. Several years later, I was perplexed as to why nobody at the time smacked me on my head with a brick to wake me up! I had fallen for the myth that I had heard from many that "lawyers made a lot of money so loans were not a problem." As my experience in life later demonstrated, this sentence was not always true, especially not in my case. Please do not misunderstand me; I know that many lawyers do earn very lucrative salaries. I am very happy for them; I am sure they have earned it; however, my own journey has been different. Someone once advised me while I was attending law school to be patient, as I would eventually see the light at the end of the tunnel. I would love to see this person again and tell them *"whoever was in charge of the electricity that powered the light at the end of the tunnel must have neglected to pay for it."* I saw no light and endured much darkness after law school. In hindsight, I can see how everything that I suffered during and after law school resulted in tremendous spiritual and emotional growth for me. I feel very blessed, despite the prolonged sufferings and the numerous dark years I endured.

Several months before departing to law school, I met a very friendly, funny man while out Salsa-dancing with some friends. His name was Tony and he had recently moved from Los Angeles. He was born and raised in Nicaragua but was naturalized United States citizen. We became very good friends and started dating. If you were paying close attention in the previous chapters, you should be saying to yourself now "*I thought she said she was not allowed to date.*" You are absolutely right. I was not. In fact, this might still come as news to my family when they read this book, but Tony and I started going out. *Sorry Mom and Dad for not telling you then, although I think you probably guessed it on your own.*

Now here is the catch. Although I was 24 years old, dating was still not allowed. In Jordan, if a man and a woman were "visually" interested in each other, they could not date. Instead, the man, accompanied by his family, went over to the woman's family to ask for her hand, without really knowing her. When the woman came out to serve coffee and dessert, the parents of the man asked for her hand saying: "*We will not drink your coffee unless we get a favorable response to our request.*" Most of the time, the parents of the woman knew in advance about the visit and its purpose, consequently a favorable response was expected, otherwise the visit would not have taken place. Rejection still happened when the visit was a surprise and the parents of the woman did not approve of the man. In this case, the man and his family refused to drink the coffee or eat the dessert, which was probably healthier in the long run. Soon after, the couple would get engaged to be married. In a sense, the engagement equaled the dating stage, with a firm commitment for marriage which is precisely why many women in the Middle East were left with no choice but to date behind their family's backs.

My parents knew and liked Tony, as he joined my family for dinner on many holiday occasions for several years; however, I always introduced him as my "friend." This was a truthful statement as he became one of my best friends, but, he was also much more. When we started dating, I never expected our relationship to survive my law school years and the long-distance factor. I was about to move to San Francisco and he was living in Sacramento. To our surprise, the relationship lasted almost five years; it was supposed to end with a happy ending, meaning marriage, but, our plans are not always God's plan and endings are not always happy. In fact, our personal ending closed tragically.

Chapter Eight

The Growing Pains of Law School

"I have the strength for everything through him who empowers me."
- Philippians 4:13

In August 1994, Tony and I were driving in his truck with my belongings to my newly-rented small studio in San Francisco; thankfully, I was able to find a place close to my university in the Richmond District. I was very excited about moving to San Francisco as I loved the City and thought I might actually enjoy it. In case you did not know, many people in California refer to San Francisco as "the City." After working for two years, I had missed the student lifestyle. I was imagining that my life there was going to be similar to the great experience I had at UC avis. That was the extent of my naïveté as nothing was further from the '1. In fact, if someone could have shown me, during my move, what was to happen in my law school experience, as well as the many years of l struggle that followed, I would have escaped from San Francisco as my legs could run.

my orientation at law school, I had to sign a paper whereby I l would not work full-time during my first year of law school. I hough I knew that financially, it would be impossible for me to comply. I thought it was an unjust expectation given my particular financial situation and under those circumstances, I could not be bound by that promise. Despite the loans I was receiving, I needed to earn some additional money for my car payments, car insurance, health insurance and part of my rent. My loans paid for all of my tuition and my books and some of my rent, but, I needed additional funds to survive the high cost of living in San Francisco. So I contacted a temporary employment agency to help me find a part-time job. I reckoned I could work in the mornings and early afternoons. I was enrolled in the evening program so my classes did not start until 3:30 P.M. every day and lasted until 9:30 P.M.

One day prior to my interview with the temp agency, since I was not familiar with the area yet, I decided to go to downtown San Francisco to see where their office was as I did not want to get lost on the interview day and be late. I took the bus downtown and after I found the address I was looking for, I proceeded to walk toward California Street. I wanted to see the building that was on the news in 1993 where a man went on a shooting rampage, killing several lawyers and innocent bystanders in one of the law firms.

As I was walking, I was approached by a man, dressed in a suit, who wanted to know my cultural background. It became clear to him from my facial reaction that I was completely taken aback by his question and approach. He continued to state that he thought I looked exotic and just wanted to know my ethnicity. To make this story short, I ended up speaking to him for about ten minutes. He found out that I was a law student and was downtown locating a temp agency where I would be interviewing the following day. Without hesitation, he took out his business card and asked me to call him as he was going to talk to his Human Resources Director about hiring me in the company where he worked. He raved about the flexibility of the hours, as they worked long days, seven days a week. He assured me that they would accommodate my law school schedule and give me health benefits. He pointed down the street to show me where the company was located. I thanked him and walked away very surprised. I did not know what to think. It was too peculiar how our conversation started and what took place. I did not know if I could trust this man. I knew I needed to pray hard about this before contacting him again.

After I prayed, I decided to call him and asked to talk directly with the Human Resources Director. I knew that by talking to the Director, I would know if this man was genuine or not. When I made my call, I was comforted to hear a friendly female voice on the other line. I interviewed the following morning for a customer service representative position; I was immediately hired for what became my occupation for the following three years while in law school. Before I move further, just in case you are wondering what happened between me and the man who got me the interview, the answer is *nothing*. He later got a decent company bonus for recruiting me. We had a professional relationship the whole time I worked there.

Over the three years of law school, my life was absolutely insane. My days and hours at work varied depending on my schedule at school. My work was flexible and I felt very blessed by that. I was exhausted juggling the demanding classes with my work.

Here is what a typical day of law school was like for me:

I woke up at 4:15 A.M., showered, had some coffee and rushed out the door. I drove my car to my university and left it in the parking garage. I then waited for the 5:30 A.M. bus that took me to downtown San Francisco. I arrived at work at 5:50 A.M. and opened the company doors to commence business at 6:00 A.M. to meet the needs of our East Coast clients. I worked from 6:00 A.M. until 2:00 P.M. with a thirty-minute lunch break. At 2:00 P.M., I walked a couple of blocks to the bus station and took the bus that dropped me off at my university at 2:45 P.M. I then proceeded to the church which was across the street from the law school. My university was a Catholic Jesuit University and had a beautiful church on campus. Every day, after work and before class, I went into the church and dropped down on my knees in prayer. My short prayer sounded like this:

"My beloved Jesus, please give me the strength to get through this day. I know there is nothing that you and I cannot do together. Please give me the graces I need to make it through the rest of the day."

After leaving the church, I proceeded directly to the university. I grabbed a quick cup of coffee and continued to my classes until 9:30 P.M. After my last class, I either went to the library until 11 P.M. or went home to study. This crazy cycle repeated every day for three years, including summers.

Two important relationships kept me alive and sane during this time. The first was with my Lord Jesus. He sustained, strengthened and carried me through every moment of my day. Only Jesus knew of each teardrop I shed during numerous nights of total exhaustion as I tried to fall asleep.

The second important relationship was with Tony. He helped me stay focused in the midst of my chaotic schedule. We spoke daily over the telephone, during every break and between classes. We often went out Salsa-dancing over the weekend, to discharge all the stress. When I danced with him, I released all my worries and anxieties. He was an extremely talented dancer and he helped me forget all my concerns, at least temporarily. Tony was very gregarious and humorous. We laughed a lot together. Overall, our relationship kept my life balanced.

On certain days when I was too overwhelmed by my hectic schedule, I would drive late at night after class to one of my favorite spots in the City. It was adjacent to what was known as the historic *Cliff House* north of Ocean Beach at the Northwest corner of San Francisco. The *Cliff House* stood on the cliff overlooking some very huge rocks in the ocean. I used to arrive at that spot consumed with anxiety and pressure. Hearing the majestic sound produced by the ocean waves as they engulfed the rocks, always gave me a tremendous sense of peace as it made me realize the grandeur of life, and how my own problems seemed like nothing in comparison.

Despite my full-time employment, I managed to work two legal internships while in law school. During that time, I worked on Saturdays and Sundays to compensate for the two days I used during the week for the internships. I interned for one semester in the law school's Civil Clinic. We dealt mostly with unlawful detainers and landlord-tenant issues. This was a great experience for me as I was fortunate to deal with a case that made it to court. The judge forced us into a settlement conference, which resolved the issue. It was a very exciting case for me filled with unbelievably memorable twists.

In addition, I interned for six months at the San Francisco District Attorney's Office. I worked specifically for the Family Violence Project. We worked mainly with victims of domestic violence and advocated for them. This was such an eye-opener experience for me. I had no idea how wide-spread and frequent domestic violence was. I was trained to deal with these issues and had my own clients. To my surprise, we had a couple of victims who only spoke Arabic. I was assigned to them and helped the assistant district attorney with the translation and interviews. In addition, I worked on a homicide study where I reviewed all the files of all the murders involving female victims in San Francisco for one particular year. The study clearly showed the majority of these murders were executed by men who were not strangers, but well known by the victims. My work was not easy as it was very emotionally draining.

Looking back, law school felt like I was being rigorously trained in a spiritual and physical boot camp. It strengthened my faith, endurance and stamina to levels beyond my imagination. I often told myself if I could survive my law school experience, I could survive anything in life. The courses at school were not the cause of hardship for me. They were definitely intellectually challenging, which felt wonderfully stimulating, however, it was the totality of my life's circumstances that made my experience so unforgettably painful.

Working full-time and going to law school full-time felt like I was on a mission to self-destruct. During my third year, I became extremely ill. I did not realize how sick I was because I had developed such a high tolerance for pain. I burned with a high fever for many days before I ended up in the emergency room with two IVs in my arms. I was depleted of all energy and was suffering from a major kidney infection. I was grateful to Tony and my close friend Wendy who drove to San Francisco around 3:00 A.M. to transport me home. The Lord always sends me help!

Nevertheless, with God's grace, Jesus and I made it through together. We graduated in May 1997. It was a triumphant day indeed, yet not particularly joyful. The California Bar Examination was looming fiercely in the background, threatening to steal any expressions of happiness or excitement.

Just in case you do not know what it entails to become a licensed lawyer in California, let me give you my very own, strongly opinionated, and critical version of the process, based on my own painful experience. I should add that most likely, many lawyers who had an easier time through law school, might disagree with me. I thoroughly respect their opinions as their experience does not reflect mine.

Even though I borrowed around $100,000 in student loans, went through three years of what I called "living hell" to get through law school, received my Juris Doctor (J.D.) degree and graduated from law school, I still could not practice law or become a lawyer. To be licensed by the State, I needed to pass the California State Bar Examination which is commonly known as the "Bar Exam." By the way, there is absolutely no alcohol involved in this bar despite what the name might suggest to you. As you can reasonably gather, I disagree with the whole process of getting licensed to become a lawyer. I can appreciate if the licensing requirements entailed six months of actual practicum or internship hours that would have benefited me by training and preparing me to do my work as a lawyer, instead of the six months I spent between taking the bar test and waiting for the results.

I had to take a class called the "Bar Course" two days after my graduation. The class lasted for six weeks. I was warned by many in law school that in order for me to have a chance in passing the bar exam, I must take the study course. In fact, I could not forget the memorable words of my bar course instructor on the first day of class. He said to us:

"You need to forget everything you learned in law school and pay close attention to what you need to learn for the bar and how you learn it. If you study for the bar exam like you studied in law school, I can almost guarantee you that you will not pass it. We will teach you everything you need to learn here to succeed and pass this exam."

I was extremely alarmed by his remarks. I thought to myself, did he just imply that my three years of law school were a complete waste of time, not to mention all my pain and agony? Wouldn't have I been smarter if I had just completely skipped law school, saved $100,000, spared myself all the suffering I endured, and just taken the bar course? That seemed more logical to me, as it appeared from this man's remarks the end result would have been identical, minus the debts and three years of suffering.

Of course, that was my wishful thinking because this would not have been possible as the State Bar of California required us to have a university law degree, from an accredited law school, to be eligible to take the bar exam. Incidentally, the bar exam lasted for three consecutive days. Each day consisted of six hours of examination.

Right after my graduation, I decided to temporarily move back to my parents' house. I could not imagine worrying about work or bills while preparing for the bar. So I took out an additional student loan to pay for the bar course and my monthly bills as I studied over the next two months.

At the end of July 1997, after countless hours of studying, I took my exam. It was 8:00 A.M. and I was already wiped out as I could not sleep the night before. My anxiety level reached such an elevated stage that my mind could not shut down to allow me the much needed sleep. I do not know how I survived the first day. I remember praying so hard for the Holy Spirit to fill me and keep me awake. With only God's grace, I survived the three days. After the grueling exam, I had to wait almost four months for the results.

At the end of November 1997, I remember logging online to check the much dreaded bar results. My whole career as a lawyer depended on them. My friend Wendy came to the house to give me support as my parents were in a church service that evening. She knew how much I suffered through law school and the bar exam. She knew I was either going to be crying hysterically or celebrating exuberantly that night. I knew she was praying for the latter. She stood next to me while the computer was retrieving the information.

I had been informed that if I passed, my name should pop up on the screen with a congratulatory remark. If I did not pass, I would get an apologetic statement without my name showing. As the screen finally processed the information, for a split of a second, my heart completely sunk in my chest as I saw a statement without my name. I remember dropping my head down between my hands as I screamed "*I did not pass.*" It was one of the most horrible moments of my life. I could not forget Wendy's voice, as she quickly responded: "*Samia, why are you saying that, look at the computer screen, your name is on it, your name just showed up.*"

I remember looking at the screen and seeing my name with a congratulatory statement. I screamed once again but this time it was a different scream. I never knew a human being was capable of experiencing such extreme emotions, only a few seconds apart. I quickly printed that screen as evidence, just in case someone at the California State Bar later changed their mind. You just never knew with these things.

I was feeling so exhilarated and joyful that I flew off my chair, ran out of the room and screamed so loud the following resonating words:

I passed! I passed! Jesus you passed! We passed! Thank you! Thank you! Thank you!

I do not know if my whole neighborhood heard me that night, but at that moment I was too euphoric to care.

I was so thankful that Jesus and I passed the bar examination on the first try. (I have a feeling Jesus has taken this exam many times with others before and after me). Usually, the average passage rate for California's exam is around 50%, if not less, as it is known to be the most difficult to pass in the whole country. For a split second, I really experienced the disappointment and upset of not passing and I feel for those who do not pass. The entire experience was so psychologically and emotionally devastating, that if I had not passed the first time, I doubt I would have had the strength to live through that heart-wrenching experience again. I admire any lawyer who was able to persevere and do it again. If you happen to be one, may the Lord bless your heart for your incredible strength and perseverance! I admire you!

Chapter Nine

The Dark Nights of My Soul

"Consider it all joy, my brothers, when you encounter various trials, for you know that the testing of your faith produces perseverance. And let perseverance be perfect, so that you may be perfect and complete, lacking in nothing... Blessed is the man who preservers in temptations, for when he has been proved he will receive the crown of life that he promised to those who love him."

- James 1: 2-4, 12

While I was waiting for my bar results after the examination, I started looking for legal jobs. I could not yet practice law but I knew many firms hired recent graduates as interns while awaiting their bar results. Since my law school was located in San Francisco, I was at a complete disadvantage when I moved back to Sacramento to study for the bar. Usually the law school's career office assisted their students in locating local firms and lawyers who were hiring recent graduates.

In Sacramento, there were two local law schools I knew of, UC Davis School of Law and McGeorge School of Law. I was already familiar with the UC Davis campus so I went there to see if I could look for job vacancies at their law school's career office. I was not familiar with the office so I innocently asked a woman who looked like she worked there for help. She looked bothered as she asked me if I was a student there. I told her I was not a student at the law school but I was an alumnus of UC Davis' undergraduate programs. She rebuked me and told me I was not allowed to use their resources as they were strictly for their own law students. She added that it was irrelevant that I had previously graduated from that university as the law school was a professional school and was a separate entity. I was in complete shock as I could not believe my ears. I felt so helpless and distraught by her lack of assistance or cooperation.

Remaining hopeful, I proceeded to McGeorge School of Law. I was not familiar with their career office either, but this time I knew better and did not dare to ask for help. I reviewed their employment board. I was able to find an advertisement by a local labor union that had a vacancy. They were soliciting recent law school graduates to work as a "Hearing Representative" in their union. I quickly jotted down the information and contacted them. I was scheduled for an interview on the following day.

My interview went very well. I was offered the position in the union; however, the position was not a staff position and offered no benefits whatsoever. They did not have any vacant staff attorney positions and were not anticipating any vacancies in the near future. Here is the worst part; the pay was only $11.00 per hour. After a total of eight years of university education, three of which were in a professional university, my first hourly pay was $11.00 per hour. *Are you shocked?* I was. I know it is hard to believe. Number "11" will have a special significance to me for as long as I live.

Nevertheless, I tried to look at my situation through positive eyes. I had not yet passed the bar exam so I could not yet look for attorney positions in law firms. Meanwhile, the experience I would gain from this position would benefit me tremendously. I would be dealing mostly with labor and employment issues which I hoped would prepare me for a career in that law field. So, I welcomed the opportunity.

I was employed there from August 1997 through March 1998. It was an invaluable experience that taught me greatly. What I enjoyed the most about working there were all the wonderful people I met. Everyone was so helpful and friendly. To my great delight, I met some amazing recent graduates from McGeorge Law School, who also worked there as Hearing Representatives. They were funny, relaxed and so down-to-earth. We all joked together about the significance of the number "11" in our lives and the horrors of the bar exam and law school. It was so therapeutic for all of us to vent about what we had experienced, each in our own way.

After I received my bar results, I started actively looking for attorney positions. I applied to countless local law firms but to no avail. It was a frustrating and demoralizing experience. Most of the law firms had stringent requirements for applicants. For example, many required the applicants to be in the top 10% or 20% of their graduating class, or to have participated in extracurricular academic activities such as Law Review or Moot Court. My reality was so different than what these law firms were seeking. Although I graduated on the top of my class in high school, graduated from UC Davis with high honors in one of my two majors, my law school experience was totally different. Of course I was not in the top 10% or 20% of my class in law school. I would be lucky if I was even in the top 50%. To be truthful, I had no idea what my class ranking was as that was the least of my concerns.

As far as I was concerned, I was just trying to survive the excruciating schedule I had. My goal in law school was to pass all my classes, to graduate successfully and then to pass the bar exam while still breathing without the assistance of an oxygen mask. I believed I successfully achieved all my goals. *Do you agree?*

I was hoping to find employment with a law firm that looked beyond the grades and class rankings. I was hoping to be hired by a firm that looked for lawyers with my well-rounded solid background, tenacious character, integrity and loyalty, multi-tasking abilities, incredible worldly experience, fluency in four languages, work ethics, jovial personality, legal internship experience and employment history which demonstrated the array of skills and adaptability that I possessed. I had worked ever since I was fourteen years old. I had held all kind of jobs while I was in high school, at UC Davis, in France and also in Law School. I do not have any memories of me not working ever since I immigrated to the United States. I always either worked full-time or part-time, summer vacations and holidays. My life was not handed to me on a silver platter. I had to work hard for everything. I am not complaining about this. I actually feel very blessed that the Lord always gave me the graces I needed. Everything I have experienced and endured helped to form my character and who I am today. For that I am eternally grateful to God. Of course, I could not see then all the blessings in disguise; I was too blinded by my utter frustrations and self-pity.

My application process lasted for several months but to no avail. I was contacted by only one law firm for an interview. Although I thought the interview went really well, I received an apology letter from them before too long. I was told in the letter I did not have enough experience. Of course I didn't! I had just passed the bar exam. It would have been impossible for me to have had any experience as a lawyer.

I was feeling very frustrated and pressured financially. I had deferred the payment of my student loans for six months after graduation. Meanwhile the balance I owed, which was over $100,000, was increasing every day as interest accrued on the principal of the loan. Thankfully, I was living at my parents' house so I did not have to worry about paying rent. Nonetheless, it was very difficult for me to move there after law school. They were still treating me as if I was a child and at times I felt like I was being suffocated.

To worsen my situation even more, my long relationship with Tony ended. I felt extremely hurt, devastated, and betrayed. Right when I thought that my life was finally going to settle down, I suddenly felt like I had nothing solid to stand on. I was crushed by the break-up. I saw all the dreams about our future vanishing before my eyes. I tried to pray but it was often too hard for me. I remember thinking to myself that I could not allow any other man to hurt me like this again. For several years, I unconsciously placed a guard around my heart to block other men from coming in. At the same time, my heart was silently hoping that Tony and I would reconcile our differences, despite the pain I was enduring.

We managed to remain "friends." In hindsight, this was a big mistake. We did not know any better at the time, as we were still emotionally immature despite both being in our late twenties. I now believe couples, in general, can remain "only" friends after a break-up if they have first allowed themselves a long period of separation to enable a healing process to occur in their hearts. Life has taught me that one of the worst things that we can do after a break-up is to jump immediately into another relationship, or to stay connected to the previous one. This is usually an indication that we are avoiding confronting the pain, which does not magically disappear because we refuse to acknowledge it. The denied pain festers within our hearts, causing us even more harm than the original wound, as we prolong the period of suffering. That is exactly what Tony and I did. Because of our insecurities and wounds, especially from our childhood fears of abandonment and rejection, we held on to our friendship, without allowing any healing time for our hearts. Trust was already broken in our relationship. It was not going to be magically restored by our "friendship." Thus, the pain and suffering endured for several years even after the official ending of the relationship.

In hindsight, although Tony and I were decent adults and thought we loved each other, I believe our hearts were undeveloped emotionally or even spiritually. We were incapable of truly loving each other since we did not truly love ourselves. Simply stated, one cannot give to others what one does not have. In life, we often seek the love or approval of others to enable us to love ourselves or to validate our own existence, which usually results in either a complete dependency on others or a twisted unhealthy notion of "love." This is usually why many people fall apart or even become suicidal after a break-up in a relationship. In reality, most human hearts are wounded before relationships even start. Because of the already existing infancy or childhood wounds of our hearts, we unintentionally project our pain and hurtful feelings on others, regardless of the type of relationship in question - whether romantic, friendly, familial or business.

To illustrate what I am saying, here is a typical example. Let us suppose that one day Tony and I had made plans to go out to dinner. It often happened that one of us was tired due to our heavy schedules. Suppose Tony, at the last minute, decided to cancel the dinner plans. Given that I had previous rejection wounds, I could be "triggered" by his cancellation as I would assume that he just did not want to be around me, but, in reality, he was truly tired. So of course, because of my previous rejection wounds, I would get upset with him and maybe even angrily hang up the phone on him. In return, remembering his own father's or mother's anger with him, he might react to my anger. As a result, we would have a simple situation unintentionally developing into a major argument between us. This type of scenario often occurs in relationships as we misinterpret a current situation and consequently project our pain and hurtful feelings onto others. Our hearts need God's healing love to stop this cycle. Although love can lead to pain, pain usually leads to spiritual and emotional growth, if we allow it. Over the following years after my break-up with Tony, I suffered a great deal, yet, because I turned to God for His healing love, these experiences allowed me to grow tremendously - emotionally and spiritually. By allowing God to heal the root of the pain in my heart, I did not suffer all those years in vain. I know now that only God's love can fill the emptiness that we feel in our hearts. Only His love can heal our pain and restore us. Only through His love within us can we truly love others unselfishly.

To help me deal with my emotional pain, my very dear friends, Vernel and Marizol, invited me to start attending the Latino youth and young adult prayer group at their parish, Immaculate Conception Church, under the authority of the Catholic Diocese of Sacramento, called *PAHIES* (***Padre,***

Hijo, Espíritu Santo); this is Spanish for "Father, Son and Holy Spirit." As a married couple, they coordinated the group together. I had never previously been involved in anything like that. They prayed the rosary, sang joyful praise songs, read the Bible, taught biblical lessons and even prayed inner-healing prayers with us. I started attending this group every Monday after my work. I began learning more about the Bible and my faith. In addition, it was very therapeutic for me as I was able to cry and allow our Lord to gently touch my broken heart. Furthermore, I was very inspired by how Vernel and Marizol lived. They had two very young daughters then and they always participated as a family. I saw so much light and love in them. The Lord Jesus was the center of their family. They truly lived their Christian faith, not just on Sundays, but every day, and it showed. Vernel and Marizol have been such a tremendous blessing to my life. They have been used as God's instruments to connect me with the Latino faith community, particularly, the Hispanic Catholic Charismatic Renewal ("CCR").[18] Even though I am Catholic, I have never previously known anything about this spiritual movement. CCR focuses on a total renewal of the person through a conversion to Jesus Christ by being open to the action of the Holy Spirit, by being filled with His gifts and charismas, and by evangelizing with power as well as growing every day in holiness as occurred on the day of Pentecost.[19] Several years later, I became very involved within this Latino faith community which opened many avenues in my life.

Despite my emotional pain from the breakup with Tony, I remained actively searching for employment; I was contacted for an interview by a

---

[18] For more information on the Catholic Charismatic Renewal, visit http://iccrs.org
[19] Acts 2: 1-4

non-profit organization that represented children in dependency hearings. Even though the pay was low, I highly valued the work they did. Children always have had a very special place in my heart. I went for an interview and hoped for the best. I did not hear back from them for almost a month. They contacted me again to schedule a second interview for Tuesday of the following week. During that weekend, one of my friends contacted me to go out Salsa-dancing. I had not been out dancing in months. She knew I was depressed because of Tony and wanted to cheer me up. While at the dance club, I ran into a friend whom I had not seen for many months. She asked me how my employment search was going. I told her I was still working for the labor union but actively looking for an attorney position in a law firm. I also shared with her that I was scheduled for a second interview for an attorney position during the following week, which sounded hopeful. She immediately told me there was a vacancy for the Human Resources Director position in the corporation where she worked. My friend added that even though it was not a lawyer position, my labor union background would help tremendously as they dealt with many employment and labor issues. My friend happened to be the vice-president of the corporation; she promised to talk to the corporation's president on Monday about me, as she knew I had another interview scheduled for Tuesday afternoon.

To my surprise, my friend contacted me on Monday and scheduled me for an interview with the president for Tuesday morning. I felt very torn within my heart. Even though the position sounded appealing to me, it was not an attorney position. After passing the bar, I was hoping to find employment in a law firm or a corporation as a lawyer, especially after all what I endured to earn it. With the exception of the interview that I had on

Tuesday, I had had no responses from any law firms. On one hand, I felt desperate to earn a regular salary with benefits. The financial burden I was carrying was already suffocating me. The payments for my student loan were to commence the following month. I had no guarantee that I would be offered the lawyer position that I was interviewing for with the non-profit organization. I knew I was not the only one who was being second-interviewed.

As I usually did, I decided to place my dilemma in God's hands. I went to church on Monday afternoon and prayed really hard for a sign from God. I asked Him to make it clear to me on Tuesday which position He had planned for me. I was seeking His will and guidance. I knew my own ego would feel better with a lawyer position. There was a certain prestige that resulted in saying that to people when they asked about my employment. Thankfully, my ego matured significantly in the past ten years.

On Tuesday morning, I interviewed with the president of the corporation. Everything went very well. To my surprise, he offered me the position immediately. I still had my other interview to attend with the nonprofit legal organization. So I proceeded there absolutely relaxed as I knew I was employed already. Even though the interview was tough as I was asked to do a legal presentation, I did very well as I was feeling self-assured after I had accepted the corporation's offer. Incidentally, ten days later they made me an offer for the job. Unfortunately, I had already started my employment with the corporation and it did not feel right for me to resign. I declined the offer as it came too late.

I commenced my new employment the following week as the Human Resources Director. I reported directly to the president of the corporation. He became my immediate supervisor. Even though it was a new position for me, the Lord guided me through everything. I was very blessed by the assistance I received from my supervisor's executive secretary. She was like an angel to me and a gift from God. She had filled in temporarily after the previous director resigned. She familiarized me with my new surroundings and especially the software that I needed to use. I worked six to seven days a week, approximately thirteen hours a day for the first five months.

Within two months, I cleaned up the entire department, got caught up on all the pending files, conducted trainings of the managers on employment and labor issues and gained the affection of most of my fellow employees. I thoroughly enjoyed working with the diverse staff. In many ways it felt like working for a family. I gave the corporation my full heart and loyalty as if I was operating my own business. Not only did I deal with Human Resources issues but I also was in charge of the entire payroll for over 200 employees, which was another full-time job by itself. I joyfully completed my tasks, without complaining and regardless of the hours it took me. The corporation became my second home.

After five months of my employment, my supervisor called me into his office. He informed me that since he was extremely impressed by my performance, he wanted to promote me to another position that had just become vacant. He told me that the Vice President who handled governmental contractual matters had resigned. He offered me the position as he felt that it was more legal in nature and more in alignment with my education and background. The responsibilities of this position included, amongst many things, ensuring that the corporation remained compliant with all the new laws and regulations related to our business in addition to managing all the government contracts.

I felt ecstatic by this offer and accepted it immediately. My supervisor informed me that he would look for a replacement for my current position. Meanwhile he asked me to continue temporarily performing my duties as the Human Resources Director while also assuming the duties of the new position. He did not mention an increase in my compensation for the new position, but I reasonably assumed that I would get a raise that reflected the increased responsibilities. Since I was in charge of payroll, unfortunately, I was exposed to the salary of the person I was replacing, which at the time, was more than two and a half times what I was earning. He also was supported by a full time executive assistant whose salary was not much less than mine. In my naïveté, I assumed that I would have a big increase in my salary, not necessarily to what he was earning, but at least seventy-five percent of it, as the person I was replacing was not a lawyer, even though he was very knowledgeable of the law. He had been employed by the corporation for less than one year when he resigned.

I immediately took on my new tasks, with less than three hours of training for this new position by the person who vacated it. He gave me enough information to get me started on my own strenuous self-teaching quest. What made this new position more challenging, was trying to learn the new responsibilities, without the support of my predecessors' executive assistant who was released from her position shortly after I assumed the job, while fulfilling the demanding requirements of the Human Resources Department, including payroll. My supervisor had promised me that this would be a temporary situation. I continued to serve in both positions for more than ten consecutive months. Without exaggeration, I worked daily, Monday through Sunday, 7:00 A.M. to 11 P.M. or midnight. If it was not for my law school boot camp experience, I would have never survived managing these dissimilar departments.

For several months, I had no pay increase or any bonus while I was performing all these tasks. My oldest brother, also a lawyer, had a long serious talk with me, out of his love and concern for me. He is extremely smart and very business-oriented. He could not understand why my supervisor had not discussed my compensation yet. My brother told me that if I were to calculate my hourly wage based on the outrageous hours I was working, I would be earning less than $8.00 per hour. Since my positions were considered "exempt" from wage and hour laws, I was not paid any overtime pay, regardless of how many hours I worked. My brother insisted that I needed to speak to my supervisor. He did not want anyone to take advantage of my hard work, loyalty and dedication.

Even though my brother made perfect sense and I agreed with him, I felt very uncomfortable discussing money matters, such as my compensation, with my supervisor. In general, I always avoided this subject with people. Two things that I completely hated and felt extremely uneasy with in life were asking for money or owing money to an acquaintance. I usually did not allow my friends to treat me or pay for me. I would always hasten to pay for them instead, which was insane as my financial situation did not give me the liberty to do that. As a result, I ended up, unintentionally, hurting my friends and myself. I knew in my heart that what I was doing was not a helpful or humble behavior. It was an issue of my heart that needed much healing. At the time, I did not know the root cause of my conduct. I assumed it resulted from either the obnoxious side of my pride or from not wanting to owe anyone any favors. I even falsely believed that if somebody was to give me something for free, they might think they had control over me. With my student loans, I began to perceive the situation differently. Even though I owed a huge amount of money, I knew that I was paying more than my fair share of interest on the loans to a personally unknown institution or a lender.

Thankfully, several years later, I received a huge healing from our Lord about this. He showed me in prayer the root cause of my behavior. It resulted from low-self esteem and a false belief system. I just did not love myself enough to know my value. I did not truly believe that I was worthwhile, despite all my credentials. Therefore, I felt unworthy of people spending money on me. The lies I believed about myself became my reality. I am very thankful to our Lord as I am in a completely different place in my life today. Even my friends now see the change.

Returning to my work situation, despite my extreme uneasiness, I finally gathered enough courage to make an appointment with my supervisor to discuss my compensation. I explained my situation and all the hours I was working. I inquired what my increased compensation would be for this position that I had been performing over the previous two months. He told me that he had not given it much thought. I gave him the salary figure that I believed I deserved to earn based on the position's responsibilities and requirements. To my complete surprise, he looked startled by the figure I mentioned.

The salary I was asking for was still significantly lower than what the person I replaced was earning. In effect, I had replaced two people and was saving the company a significant amount of money even if they were to pay me the salary I was requesting. My supervisor responded that he needed to think about the amount I requested and would get back to me with his response.

The following day, he called me into his office. He informed me that he disagreed with the amount I was asking. He counter-offered me with a much lower number. This new amount was 50% of the salary of the person I replaced. In addition, I was still performing duties of the Human Resources Director. I was not replaced in that department for nine months. I was not compensated any additional money for all the work I did there.

I was devastated by his response. I do not know how I managed to hold in my burning tears of disappointment and extreme humiliation. After the outrageous hours I had worked and the loyalty I showed the corporation, I felt like my supervisor had just completely shattered my morale. I felt like I had no choice but to accept his counter-offer. Otherwise, my only other option was to resign. At that point this option seemed unfeasible with all my monthly bills, especially the high student loan amounts I was paying. I was counting on this compensation increase to be able to move out of my parents' house. All my belongings were in storage and I lived in a very small bedroom in my parents' home. I could barely move in the room as I had kept some boxes filled with essential books and documents all around the floor. The temporary situation had already surpassed sixteen months and ended up lasting a total of four years! My new paycheck was not sufficient for me to pay my monthly bills and be able to rent an apartment, or even a bedroom with someone else. Despite my crushed spirit, I continued my duties and responsibilities, performing them with excellence, gaining the praise of all our business associates, and the regulatory attorneys with whom I dealt.

It is important to highlight that the Middle Eastern culture I came from had contributed greatly to my acceptance of my work situation. My childhood experiences, the unworthiness and diminished value I felt about myself, all the cultural lies I believed, collaborated in falsely confirming I "deserved" my hopeless situation.

I remained in this stagnant state for four years. Despite what superficially appeared to others as a prestigious, successful career, underneath, I was feeling like a complete failure. Every day was a battle for me. I felt like I was swimming upwards just to survive. I never saw any rewards for all my years of hard work. As soon as my check came in, the money went out to pay for my loans and other debts, such as my car payment, car insurance and credit card bills that I incurred during law school to supplement my loans. My dreams in life such as getting married, having a family and buying a house, completely evaporated. The words spoken to me by one of my friend's mother, after my graduation from law school, constantly echoed in my ears as a reminder of my bleak destiny: *"Samia, who will marry you with all your student loans?! That is a big burden for anyone."*

When I went to law school, I was driven by my dream to help people. I wanted to be a voice for the voiceless. Having grown up without any rights in a country where I lived in fear of speaking out, I was thrilled to become a lawyer in a country with such unmatched constitutional rights. After becoming a lawyer, the reality of my life transformed my aspirations into unattainable dreams. My new goal in life became having a balance of zero "0." I just wanted to live debt-free. My dreams were not the typical American dreams of having a family with two children, owning a home and driving a sports utility vehicle. I lived in slavery to my loans. Financially, I was worse off after a total of eight years of university education than I was when I graduated from high school. I felt that having gone to law school destroyed my life. With all the struggles surrounding my law school education and career, I could not help but conclude that the legal profession was not made for people like me, who came from humble backgrounds. It was made for wealthy people who could afford it and finance it. Somehow, I must have accidentally slipped through the system.

By the end of December 2000, I hit rock bottom in every way possible. My world was collapsing. I was in total darkness. I did not see any glimmer of light to give me the slightest hope. I fell into a deep depression and was heading toward utter despair. I felt like I had failed in every way possible. I was thirty-one years old, still living with my parents. I had sunk into a deep financial hole and could not find a way out of it. I failed with my decision about my education. I felt I was severely underpaid and undervalued by my supervisor at work. I could not see a way to move out or gain my independence. I failed in my relationship with Tony. I even felt betrayed by a close friend. I could not understand why God allowed this to happen to me. I thought He loved me. I thought He guided me through the whole process. I prayed hard before going to law school to determine if this was His will. I thought He showed me clearly that law school was the path for me. Did I just misunderstand His signs? Did He rejoice in all my suffering?

Out of my complete despair, I decided to confront God about my desolate state. I went to the local Catholic Cathedral of the Blessed Sacrament in downtown Sacramento. I knew it was always open during the day. It was my favorite place of prayer. I dropped down on my knees and was feeling so hurt, so angry, so betrayed, and so hopeless. I silently cried out to Him about all my feelings. I told Him that I had trusted Him. I could barely survive each passing day. I smiled at people around me but my heart was broken and bleeding profusely. I reminded Him about Medjugorje and how I had felt a strong call from Him to do something special with my life. I knew what I experienced in Medjugorje was very real. I wanted Him to show me where I went wrong along the path. I asked Him why He planted such a strong desire in my heart for Medjugorje without giving me the financial means to go back there again.

I remember weeping bitterly and passionately for a long time. I asked Him why He had abandoned me when I needed Him the most. Finally, I told our Lord that I could not handle my life anymore. I saw no future for myself. I saw no hope. I informed Him that I was appreciative of the life He had given me but I was ready to go. I told Him that I did not believe in suicide because I knew it would offend Him, but, He could choose any method He preferred to take me to my heavenly home. I begged Him to take me home!

As my sobbing quieted down, I unexpectedly heard a clear voice, speaking gently from within my heart:

You are finally surrendering your whole life to Me. You are finally releasing your need to be in control. Let go and allow Me. Be patient.

Immediately, a complete sense of peace consumed me. I sensed a dim light shining through my darkness, a ray of hope penetrating my soul. At that instant, I knew beyond a doubt that the Lord Jesus was speaking to my heart. He had never abandoned me. He was just asking me to let go of my control and be patient.

Chapter Ten

My Path to Inner-Healing

"Come to me, all you who labor and are burdened, and I will give you rest. Take my yoke upon you and learn from me, for I am meek and humble of heart; and you will find rest for yourselves. For my yoke is easy, and my burden light."

- Mathew 11:28-30

L eading such a hectic life, I often had limited patience. Patience had been one of my weakest virtues. My time was valuable; I did not know how to wait for things. I was a person who needed to be in control of my life, my tasks and my time. I had to be very well-organized and detailed to survive the insane life to which I had become accustomed.

Surprisingly, I did not have to wait too long for our Lord's words *"be patient"* to bear fruits in my life. During the first week of 2001, I received a letter from a lender promising to cut my student loan payments by half if I consolidated my federal loans for a fixed interest rate. My loans would be refinanced over thirty years, instead of the existing ten years. Even though the total balance due would almost triple by the end of the period, at that moment I did not care. I was just trying to survive. As I was not anticipating a raise, this seemed to be my only chance to get a financial break. I needed to move out on my own. I loved my parents' dearly, but at that point in my life, I believed that it would be more beneficial for our relationship if I moved out. I needed my own space and independence.

I submitted my loan consolidation application. Within a couple of months, the transaction was fully completed. My loan payments were reduced to half, which enabled me to rent my own apartment. Of course, initially, my parents were not pleased with the news. As you recall, it was not customary for a single Middle Eastern woman to live on her own in the same city as her parents. I told my parents that I had no interest in what other people from the culture would say as they were neither paying my bills nor alleviating any of my excruciating pain. For the first time in my life, I felt liberated from the judgmental structure of the society.

In March 2001, I rented my first apartment in Sacramento. This became my "own place." I was yearning to have something that I called my own. Even though it was just a rental, it was mine, with my own furniture, bathroom, dishes and even guests. There was such a liberating feeling in that. I was intellectually aware that I had accomplished much through my eight years of university education. It was not something tangible that I could touch or perceive. Certainly, I had not received any financial rewards from it, especially with my low salary and the sizzling loans in the background.

As soon as I moved into my new place, my attitude and demeanor began an upward swing. My gregarious and cheerful personality resurfaced. Through my cherished friend Rasmiya, I had reconnected socially with many of my Arab-American friends. While I was in my relationship with Tony, I mostly socialized with Tony's friends who were from Latino backgrounds. I became so adjusted to their culture that it felt natural to me. I even started attending Mass and Catholic spiritual conferences in Spanish. Ironically, after my breakup with Tony, I felt uneasy being around many Middle Eastern people, perhaps due to my own fears of the cultural structure. Thankfully, my friend Rasmiya was very helpful in my transition. In a sense, my deeply embedded childhood wounds were often triggered when I was in my Middle Eastern culture. Looking back, I believe my full immersion in Tony's Latino culture was partially due to my efforts to evade my own. I was avoiding facing my own childhood wounds.

To my delighted surprise, I had an amazingly wonderful time with my new Middle Eastern friends. I felt free to be myself around them. I was impressed by their open-mindedness. We joyfully reminisced over many childhood memories, old movies, songs, jokes and cultural food. We even formed a wonderful folkloric dance troupe, dancing *"dabke."* We were invited to perform at different cultural events in Sacramento and San Francisco.

Through my new friendships, I met a new Lebanese friend who particularly impacted my life. He was brilliant and possessed exceptional spiritual depth and connectedness. Even though he was raised Muslim as a child, our spiritual connection went deeper than the labels of our religions. He was one of God's special instruments to help me turn toward my heart and look deeply within myself. He challenged me intellectually and spiritually in ways that nobody else had done before. He candidly pointed out to me that I did not value or love myself. He also cautioned me that I had never let go of Tony, despite the breakup. As a result I had completely shut off my heart, preventing anyone else from loving me, including God! He advised me to seek professional help in healing this central wound in my heart which impeded me from moving forward to where God wanted to lead me with my life's journey.

Struck by what my friend told me, I shared with a close friend the substance of our discussion. She had known me for many years and I trusted her opinion. She told me that she agreed with him that I had never received inner-healing about my breakup with Tony. My friend added that I had not been able to give others a chance, as I had not completely released Tony from my heart. She suggested that I join her in her monthly Christian-based group therapy led by Dr. Serafina Anfuso, PhD, M.F.T. ("Marriage Family Therapist"). Serafina was the Director of Joshua Ministries, a professional group of psychotherapists dedicated to assisting people on their inner-healing journey, to finding themselves and their Creator. Her international ministry lasted for over thirty-five years. In addition, Serafina offered retreats, workshops, individual and group therapy in English and in Spanish. She had authored books, videos, audios and TV programs. Serafina also developed *Restoration Therapy*[20] as led and inspired by the Lord Jesus. A devout Catholic, Serafina often stated that the Lord taught her what to do. She was very well versed in the Bible and her therapy was Christian-based. My friend highly praised Serafina's techniques, especially the educational aspect of her therapy. At the time, Serafina's groups were filled and she was not accepting any new people. My friend assured me that she would ask her to give me a chance to join.

I initially resisted and declined, falsely believing that I had no issues in my life that needed therapy. Like many, I was raised in a culture that

---

[20] Anfuso, Serafina. *Restoration Therapy – From Deception towards Wholeness.* Joshua Ministries, 2001.

attached negative connotations to therapy or counseling. I often heard when I was growing up that *"therapy was for crazy people."* After my experience of six years of group and individual therapy, I can now say that precisely the opposite of that might be more accurate. I was crazy not to be in therapy. I was in complete denial about all the issues I had as the result of my childhood hurts. I now believe it is impossible to live in this world and not have it affect us negatively in one way or another. Getting emotionally wounded is the natural byproduct of being alive in a fallen world populated by imperfect sinful humanity. It is a certainty that our heart will get emotionally hurt along the way. It takes tremendous courage to face our past, especially the childhood memories that we struggle hard to forget or block.

To my surprise, Serafina accepted that I attend one group, in July 2001, to see if I would fit in with the others. As soon as I met Serafina and heard her speak, something in my heart told me that she was going to be very significant in my life. I listened to her and was impressed by her wisdom and authority. She instructed me that her therapy was called *"Restoration Therapy."* To be in the group, I had to follow her "No JAB Rule." That meant that I could not *judge* others in the group, give them *advice*, or *blame* them for anything. The purpose of this rule was to create a safe environment for everyone involved.

She then proceeded to explain what *Restoration Therapy* was all about. In a nutshell, it is based on the following beliefs:
- Unresolved emotions and negative beliefs from childhood control our lives, how we see ourselves, others and God.
- Childhood hurts and traumas that sometimes begin as far back as the womb create rage, shame and grief in us.

- Healing comes when we face the truth about our families of origin, forgive them and also forgive ourselves.

- Restoration is the process of beginning to believe in ourselves as worthy, competent, loving and productive human beings.

Serafina discussed many topics which fascinated me. She talked about the importance of bonding with one's mother and father and the resulting shame and addictive behaviors that would be produced from the lack of bonding. She discussed spiritual bondage which happened through deception and denial, due to the lies we internalized in the beginning of our lives. These lies revolved around our identity: who we were, why we were here on earth and what we deserved in life. She discussed the cultural wounds, the teacher wounds and how they affected us. She talked about false beliefs, curses, vows and their effects on our lives. Serafina thoroughly discussed the concept of "false self" that she called "the spacesuit." She stated that we, as children, created "spacesuits" as protective shields to survive the hostile world around us. Our spacesuits served us by covering up all the shame we carried within us, that resulted from childhood wounds caused by our families, schools, churches and neighborhoods.

What truly impressed me about Serafina was her openness about her life and her own healing journey. She used stories from her childhood and adolescence to illustrate to us how our hearts got wounded in life. I was impressed by her close connection to our Lord Jesus and the way she followed His guidance during the session. She often shared with us what the Lord was telling her or instructing her to do. That was the first time that I met someone who claimed to converse with the Lord. Out of my ignorance, I did not know that was possible. At that time, I had spoken to God in prayer but never waited to hear back from Him. I naively assumed prayer was a one-way conversation, we talked and God listened.

A significant amount of praying occurred during group sessions to help in the inner-healing process. In fact, several months after I joined the group, Serafina added a Catholic priest, Father Thomas, to Joshua Ministries. Father Thomas significantly contributed to group sessions by celebrating Mass there. He privately heard group members' confessions and administered other sacraments as needed. Father Thomas also became a very significant person in my life soon after.

I immediately identified with many topics that Serafina explained. As she spoke and prayed during the group, I could not help but thank God for leading me to her. My heart was elated as I felt I had come "home."

Serafina and the rest of the group felt comfortable with me and I was invited to join their monthly meetings. I was informed that they were planning their annual retreat in Puerto Vallarta, Mexico, at the end of September of 2001. She mentioned the cost, which was fairly cheap as it was a group rate. She asked me if I wanted to join them. Something in my heart shouted *"YES."* Even though I did not have the extra money to go at the time, I knew in my heart that I had to go. I accepted and decided to charge the trip on my credit card.

In August 2001, Serafina asked me if I would be interested in getting trained as a lay prayer minister in something called *"Theophostic Prayer Ministry."* Serafina had attended conferences about this ministry and was impressed by their prayer approach as it did not require a licensed therapist to administer it. Any trained Christian lay person could do it as it was a prayer ministry centered on healing through Jesus Christ. The word *"Theo"* is a

Greek word for "God" and "*Phostic*" means "light." The Ministry's website[21] defines it as follows: *"It is a ministry of prayer that is Christ-centered and God-reliant for its direction and outcome. Simply stated, it is encouraging a person to discover and expose what he believes that is a falsehood; and then encouraging him to have an encounter with Jesus Christ through prayer, thus allowing the Lord to reveal His truth to the wounded person's heart and mind. It is not about advice giving, diagnosing problems, or sharing opinions or insight. It is about allowing a person to have a personal encounter with the Lord Jesus in the midst of the person's emotional pain."*

I was interested in learning more about this prayer ministry. Therefore, within a month of joining Serafina's group, I read the manual, watched the training videos and attended conferences to get trained. By the end of 2001, I was certified as a lay prayer minister. To be certified, I was required to receive first many hours of prayer ministry myself. I had to be on my own healing journey first, which was marvelous for me.

At the end of September 2001, I attended the retreat in Puerto Vallarta, Mexico. Originally, sixty people from around the country signed up to attend this retreat, but, as a result of the horrific events of September 11, 2001, the majority of the people canceled with the exception of four - myself and three other people. Lourdes[22] was one of the remaining three. The trip was filled with incredible healings for all of us. One particular thing that Serafina told me during the retreat stuck to my mind. While she was talking to another person, she unexpectedly turned to me, looked me straight in the eye and told

---

[21] www.theophostic.com
[22] Lourdes gave me permission to use her name as the names of group members were usually held confidential to protect their privacy.

me these memorable words: *"Samia you are chosen; you are here to get your tools."*

I was stunned by her words. I asked her why she said these words to me. Her only response was: *"The Lord just revealed that to me."*

My eyes watered up. Even though I did not understand what her words clearly meant or implicated, they took me back to my experience in Medjugorje eleven years prior to that. I clearly remembered the strong call I felt in my heart. As my life unfolded, it became clear that my call was not to become a nun or join a religious order. There was something else that the Lord was calling me to do as a lay person. At that moment, the Lord once again was speaking to me through Serafina. He wanted me to recognize Serafina's role in my life's mission. What was becoming obvious to me though was that the Lord was first asking me to start my inner-healing process. At the same time, the Lord, through Serafina, was teaching me the principles of inner-healing; He also was giving me laity tools, through the prayer ministry, to be able to help others on their inner-healing journey.

While in Puerto Vallarta, I also met and received my first private therapy session from Alysa, M.F.T. Alysa was the Associate Director of Joshua Ministries and a close friend of Serafina's. She is a licensed psychotherapist in private practice. She leads *Restoration Therapy* groups and supervises lay prayer ministers in Theophostic Prayer Ministry. In addition, she co-authored a book with Serafina. Due to Serafina's sudden terminal illness in the year 2004, Serafina asked Alysa to take over her therapy groups.

To the great sadness of hundreds of people whose lives had been immensely and positively affected by Serafina's ministry, she passed away into eternal life on January 19, 2006. I am very grateful for her life and all the lessons she taught me.

Alysa also has been an incredible gift to me from God. She is probably one of the most emotionally-healed people I know on earth. Even though she is a therapist herself, she continues the path of her own healing journey. As a result, she is a clean vessel for the Lord's usage. I believe the Lord speaks to her clearly. I trust her discernment as it has not failed me.

Just to illustrate to you how bound we are by our false belief system and the lies we believe about ourselves, I feel the need to share with you some of the healings I have received during my private session with Alysa in Puerto Vallarta. Even though the session lasted only two hours, the healings I received from Our Lord Jesus will last a lifetime. His truth in specific memories set me free from my lies.

In inner-healing prayer ministry, typically after the opening prayer, the session started with identifying the person's present emotions. Feelings are extremely important as they expose our beliefs about ourselves and others. I had a range of feelings during the session. My breakup with Tony triggered a lot of my insecurities (false beliefs) about myself. I felt ashamed of myself. I felt ugly and unlovable. I felt stupid. My first torturing thought after the breakup was *"there must be something wrong with me, maybe I was not pretty enough or good enough."* In the session, I felt so ashamed about myself and particularly my looks. Alysa asked me to embrace the feeling and just to allow the Lord Jesus to give me the graces needed to go back to the root of it, the first time I ever felt like this. Amazingly, within seconds, the Lord showed me two specific incidents from my childhood, one after the other.

In the first incident, I was about five or six years old. I saw myself with my mother visiting distant relatives. I clearly remembered one of the relatives' adult daughters saying in front of me the following words: "*The boys are so handsome, but the girl* (meaning me) *is dark-colored.*" I remembered hearing these words and immediately internalized her statement in the worst way possible. I was ugly. My skin color was inferior. In order to be pretty, I needed to be lighter. As a result, I frequently asked my mother questions such as: *Would my skin get lighter if I rubbed plain yogurt on it? Would it be lighter if I avoided exposure to the sun? Would my color change again to be light, because you once mentioned that I was very light when I was born and that my color changed the second week after my birth.* At that point, my mother realized that I had a problem with the color of my skin which had been created by the relative's comment. My mother told me to ignore the woman and her remark and not to think about it, assuring me that first, I was beautiful and second, beauty was not bound to one's skin color. The damage was already done and my mother's efforts could not free me from the lies and misinterpretations that I had already believed as a result of the woman's statement.

Alysa invited Jesus into my painful memory. Even though I did not hear an audible voice of the Lord, He spoke to my heart and told me that the color of my skin was pretty. He designed it. The young woman who spoke those words to me had her own issues with skin color. From that moment, I felt peaceful with that memory; however, the Lord was showing me there was still another important incident related to my feelings.

Another memory that I had completely forgotten surfaced quickly to my mind. I was in second grade in Jordan. Most likely I had blocked the memory to survive the excruciating pain. I was sitting in my art class, barely seven years old. It was a hot summer day. I had awakened that morning with a severe skin rash in reaction to mosquito bites. My skin was very sensitive and appealed to unmerciful insects. Embarrassed to go to school that morning in my summer uniform, I wore my heavy long-sleeved sweater to cover the visible rash. My teacher noticed me in my sweater. She stopped her lecture and approached me in front of all the other students in the class. She asked me why I was wearing a sweater. The eyes of all the boys and the girls in the classroom were fixed on me. I told her that I just wanted to wear a sweater. She then noticed some of the rash I had on my hands. She inquired about it. I was feeling so embarrassed that I froze and could not respond. She proceeded to pull up my sweater's sleeves to look at my arms. She informed me in a loud voice that I had a rash all over my arms, as if I did not know that already. She then continued to check on my neck and upper back to see if the rash had spread there also. Suddenly, all the students left their seats and approached me to look at my rash. They instantly reacted with loud noises and phrases indicating severe disgust. They immediately distanced themselves from me as if I were a contagious monster. I was devastated by everyone's reaction, especially the boys. I had never felt so humiliated in my life. I wished a hole would immediately open up and swallow me. I felt extremely ashamed as I believed I was ugly and unattractive.

As I recounted the story to Alysa, I was weeping fervently as I relived that painful moment. Alysa then invited Jesus into my memory so that I could receive His truth about the lies I had internalized. Jesus once again spoke to my heart. He showed me that I had had only a basic skin rash. Despite my classmates' reaction, there was nothing ugly about me. These were children and did not know any better then. He also showed that my teacher had not reacted in the correct manner with me. It was not my fault. Instantly, I felt peace in my heart and my memory. I stopped crying and felt tremendous light around me. I now *love* my skin color and *love* the way the Lord has carefully designed everything about me.

As my session continued, I struggled with the feeling of stupidity. I thought I could not understand things as easily as everyone else around me. Even though I had three university degrees, including a Juris Doctor of Law, spoke four languages fluently, I still believed I was not smart. I knew that this belief did not make any logical sense. Everyone around me constantly praised me for my intelligence. It did not matter what others said or what I kept on repeating to myself, deep down within me, I did not believe I was smart. Other people's truth, or my own repetition of the truth, did not release me from my lies. Repeating the positive affirmations of others did not work for me. I knew this practice might work for someone else, but for me, the repetition of affirmations just masked my lies. I believed I needed to work extra-hard to make up for my lack of intelligence. My lies shaped my own reality.

Alysa asked me to embrace my feeling and allow the Lord Jesus to give me the graces needed to go to the root of my lies. In a few seconds, I saw myself sitting in my second grade science class. The teacher was talking about the various benefits and qualities of oxygen and she said that oxygen was a very "good" combustible element in air. She then asked questions about the topic. I saw all of my classmates' hands instantly go up to respond. I was the only one who did not raise my hand as I was still pondering the frightening information which was just delivered by the teacher. At the moment, I believed I was stupid. I was the only one who did not have the answer. I believed I must have been slower than everyone else in the class.

When I returned home from school, my mother started helping me and my brothers' with our homework. As she assisted me, I asked her whether it was true that oxygen was a "good" combustible element. She answered positively, to which I responded with fearful tone: "*But why?*" My mother could not comprehend my questioning reaction and she tried to explain the subject to me in a scientific way. There was nothing wrong with that, I know that now, but then, her explanation made no sense to me. After diligent and lengthy efforts by my mother to help me understand the material, I kept anxiously repeating the same question: "*But why?*" Finally my mother became frustrated with my inability to grasp that oxygen was a "good" combustible element. Not knowing what else she could do, she stated emphatically: "*Just accept it as a fact and you don't have to know why.*" I started crying wholeheartedly, and my mother was at loss since she could not fathom the depth of my thinking. She said to me: "*Tell me, why are you crying? I don't understand.*" I replied saying: "*Since oxygen is a "good" combustible element, then every time there is a small fire anywhere, it is going to grow bigger and bigger.*" Yet my mother could not see what was beyond my words, and she said: "*Yes! This could happen.*" I was more troubled by her affirmation. In my mind, the growth of a fire into a disastrous stage was inevitable due to the presence of oxygen everywhere in the air. I responded: "*Houses will burn and people will die.*" Though my mother understood then what I was thinking and why I cried, she was still unable to reason how my mind was addressing the consequences of the combustible quality of oxygen rather than processing the scientific side of it. She was convinced that she could no longer help me and proceeded to help my brothers with their homework. Furthermore, after that incident, my mother was determined that she was incapable of helping me with my homework and she did not want to upset me anymore. Thus, she decided that she should stop helping me and my brothers with our homework. She told us that we should be more responsible and rely on ourselves, except when her help was badly needed. I became convinced that I had to be stupid. I made a decision then to study harder to teach myself and even though it was a painful process for me, I began to excel in all my classes.

We invited the Lord Jesus into my two memories to receive His truth. He showed me that just because all the students raised their hands during class, it did not mean they all knew the right answer. Most of them had the wrong answer and felt the pressure to raise their hand in imitation of the rest. That did not mean they were smarter than I was. I was just honest by not raising my hand. He then showed me that he had given me a *different* way of looking at things. This was why I could not understand my mother's or my teacher's explanation. Being different did not mean being less. He created me like that. He then showed me how, when I started teaching myself, I was able to excel to the top of my class. I would not have been able to accomplish that if I had not been smart. Instantly, I felt peaceful and happy. I embraced my *new* way of thinking. For the first time in my life, I really believed I was smart.

That day, I began a deeper and more intimate relationship with my Lord Jesus. He was healing me in the midst of my emotional pain, incident after incident. I have had many other sessions since then, probably hundreds of hours, over the past six years. I have gone into countless memories of my early childhood. Jesus always came through with His freeing truth dispelling the lies and renewing my mind. As my lies and misinterpretations from my past were being nullified, my present reality began changing. Furthermore, the more shame I discarded, the more I started loving myself. Every day, I moved one step closer to becoming the person that God created me to be, His authentic and beloved daughter.

As I heal, I am learning to genuinely forgive with all my heart. In fact, I have become more compassionate of others, especially the ones who have hurt me. By no means am I justifying their behavior, but the Lord has shown me that people hurt us because they also have been injured in a similar manner. They are functioning in the world through their own false belief systems and wounded hearts. Of course, they need to make the choice to heal instead of continuing their hurtful behavior.

When we hold on to anger or refuse to forgive others in our hearts, we end up hurting ourselves. We keep ourselves held in bondage. It is as if we drink the poison that we have intended to give to the one who hurt us. As a result, we block God's love from flowing into our hearts. Light and darkness cannot coexist. If we allow God's light to come into the darkness, the darkness must dissipate; however, the light cannot come in if we block the entrance to our heart with our hatred, anger or unforgiveness. I am convinced that we hold on to them because of our false beliefs. Maybe our anger was justified when we were children because through our anger we were able to survive the trauma, but, as adults, the anger does not serve its purpose anymore. It has a reverse effect later on in our life. Anger, lack of forgiveness and hatred fester in our hearts and become cancerous to our souls, slowly affecting the condition of our physical bodies. I believe that many physical illnesses today result directly from the anger, hatred and unforgiveness that people hold in their hearts.

In addition, I have ministered to hundreds of people over the past six years, spending countless hours in prayer with them. My ministry included males, females, children, teenagers, young adults, middle-aged adults and elderly people from all walks of life, from *different* religions and various economic backgrounds. *If the person is willing,* Jesus never fails to show up. He heals people with His *Truth* and *Love.* He has never discriminated against anyone. He loves everyone the same, regardless of the person's religion or creed. I have witnessed how He has changed my life and the lives of hundreds of others. He is really as alive today as He was 2000 years ago. He just works in a different capacity than He did then. His power is as potent as ever. I have learned through my own healing journey, and also through my ministry to others, that the more healed our hearts become, the more we are able to experience God's immense love for us.

In Chapter Fifteen, I will share with you *in depth* what I have learned about the source of all these lies we believe about ourselves. I will also explain how they keep us in bondage if we do not turn to God to receive His liberating and healing truth.

Chapter Eleven

The Reawakening of My Soul

"They that hope in the Lord will renew their strength, they will soar as with eagles' wings; they will run and not grow weary, walk and not grow faint."
- Isaiah 40: 31

The year 2001 was monumental in my life. Indeed, the Lord resurrected me from the pit of despair I had sunk into at the close of 2000. Not only did He fully launch my inner-healing journey, He also reactivated the dormant "call" in my heart that I had felt in Medjugorje eleven years prior. The memories remained fixed in the back of my mind. Over the years, I often wondered why I had that unforgettable experience at the age of twenty. What was the significance of that burning "call" I felt from God while I was there? Why was He making me wait so long to find the answers?

As I look back at my life, I now understand the wisdom behind the waiting years. When I went to Medjugorje in 1990, I was very naïve, lacking real life experience. Although I was known as "book-smart," I was far away from being "street-smart" because I had been very sheltered most of my life. When I returned to the United States in 1990, many events took place in my life which shaped my character. I was being prepared for my life's mission in ways unforeseeable to me. No time was ever wasted in my life. Through the Blessed Virgin Mary's apparitions in Medjugorje, the Lord Jesus planted the seed in my heart. The seed was watered and nourished through twelve years of real life experience. During these years, despite the joyful times, I endured much hardship. My character and soul were maturing through the excruciating hard work and advanced levels of education. The Lord exposed me to many different cultures. I even became fluent in Spanish, a language that I previously had not planned to study. All these skills are now serving their purpose.

When the time was ripe for me to return to Medjugorje, the Blessed Virgin Mary's invitation was loud and clear. The "call" that I felt inside my heart in 1990 was being revived; I felt it very strongly. Suddenly, people appeared in my life who found out about my first visit to Medjugorje. Without any suggestion from me, they genuinely wanted to hear all about my experience there.

One night in September 2001, I could not fall asleep; I was obsessively thinking about Medjugorje. I got up at 2:30 in the morning. I went to my computer and started doing some research on the internet. I wanted to get updated on what had been happening in Medjugorje since I last visited. I was elated to find the International Internet Prayer Group ("IIPG") website.[23] I immediately joined it. The purpose of this prayer group, which then had around 1500 members from all over the world, was to provide mutual support in living and following the messages of Medjugorje as guided by our Blessed Mother Mary through the visionary Ivan Dragicevic. Amazingly, after I joined the group, a series of events started unfolding that prepared me

---

[23] http://www.iipg-queenofpeace.org

to take my first trip back to Medjugorje; I went on an organized pilgrimage with the Prayer Group IIPG in June 2002. I also returned to Medjugorje with other groups in 2003, 2004 and 2005.

The same week I joined the IIPG, I got an e-mail from the prayer group that there would be a conference about Medjugorje in the city where I lived, during that upcoming weekend. One of the visionaries, Marija Pavlovic-Lunetti, was invited to speak. This definitely could not have been a mere coincidence. I attended the conference and for one weekend, I felt like I was back in Medjugorje. My heart was in ecstasy.

Within a month following the conference, four different people, from different nationalities and religions, gifted me with religious articles all pertaining to the Blessed Virgin Mary! This had never previously happened to me. The Blessed Virgin Mary was speaking to me clearly. I was truly overwhelmed and very humbled by her maternal love for me. Moreover, she was giving me a very clear message that she was everyone's mother, regardless of nationality, creed or religion.

Medjugorje became fully alive in my life. The prayer group provided me with my daily spiritual vitamins to enable me to live the Blessed Virgin Mary's messages. Although I received the e-mails concerning the annual prayer group pilgrimage, I knew that I could not afford it due to the tremendous debt of student loans. I still went down on my knees and prayed and asked our Lord to help me and show me if His mother was truly inviting me to go back. If she was, I asked the Lord to provide me with the financial means to do it.

During the course of these incidences, two very noteworthy events happened that affected my life, first emotionally and then spiritually. The first one resulted from the atrocious events that occurred on September 11, 2001. When I first learned of the news, I was horrified. I could not believe what I was watching on live television. That was the first time I saw so much pure evil unveiled before the eyes of the world. As I was praying for all the victims in the two towers, I was also dreading the thought that the monstrous perpetrators could be Middle Eastern terrorists. Like most Arab-Americans living in the United States, I was praying fervently that they would not be of my ethnicity. To my great devastation, they were. These demonic acts adversely affected me both as an American citizen and also as an Arab-American, due to the backlash that unsurprisingly followed. I could not fathom how anyone could contain so much hatred, so much pure evil. The worst part, it was all done in God's name. I was appalled to see the devil, Satan, using people's free will to cause massive destruction of life in the name of God. How could any human heart be so hardened by the devil's blatant and blasphemous lies?

Consequently, through the suggestion of my close friend Lourdes, we decided to fight back, not through earthly weapons, but through spiritual ones. We recalled the words of St. Paul in his letter to the Ephesians when he said: *"Put on the armor of God so that you may be able to stand firm against the tactics of the devil. For our struggle is not with flesh and blood but with the principalities, with the powers, with the world rulers of this present darkness, with the evil spirits in the heavens."*[24]

I met three times a week with my friends Lourdes, Wendy and a fourth friend at the Catholic Cathedral in Sacramento - the Cathedral of the Blessed Sacrament - to pray at noon. We first attended daily Mass; then we spent

---

[24] Ephesians 6: 11-12

thirty minutes praying against the demonic forces in the world and pleading for God's Mercy and Peace. We specifically prayed a prayer called the *"Chaplet of Divine Mercy"*[25] asking our Lord to cover the world with His mercy and love. We continued these prayerful meetings for eight consecutive months until the four of us departed together on a trip to Medjugorje. These prayerful meetings bore tremendous visible fruits in our lives. The four of us were strengthened spiritually; we grew much closer to God. In fact, on December 8, 2001, I consecrated my life completely to serve our Lord Jesus through our Blessed Mother Mary, following a period of thirty-three days of spiritual exercises in accordance to the teachings of St. Louis de Montfort.[26]

The second shockingly devastating event that occurred in my life took place on February 24, 2002. I was attending a local inner-healing weekend retreat with Serafina. I had been feeling extremely odd throughout the weekend. I felt a detachment in my spirit that I had never experienced before. Something inside of me felt "dead." I remember Serafina asking me how I was feeling during the retreat. I answered her that I had no feelings. It was unusual for me to make such a statement. I am usually very emotionally connected.

At the end of the retreat, I listened to my mobile telephone's voicemail messages. As soon as I heard my first message, I collapsed on the ground while screaming loudly *"NO!!!"* My friend Lourdes, who was also at the retreat, came running out to me. I told her that I thought I misunderstood the

---

[25] Diary of Saint Maria Faustina Kowalska, *Divine Mercy in My Soul.* Marian Press 2005. To obtain further information on the Chaplet of Divine Mercy, please visit: www.ewtn.com/devotionals/mercy/mmap.htm

[26] Louis de Montfort and Frederick Faber. *True Devotion to Mary.* Tan Books and Publishers, Nov. 1985

message. It could not be true. It was a message in Spanish from Tony's sister, who lived in Utah. She left a lengthy message asking me to urgently return her call. Her message ended with a tearful voice uttering these devastating words: "*Tony had a car accident around noon today and he died.*" A drunk-driver had swerved into Tony's freeway lane killing him instantly in a head-on collision.

Instantaneously, I felt that my heart stopped beating, as if it had skipped several beats at that moment. I screamed and cried hysterically. I lost all sense of reality. This could not be true. He had left on a five-week vacation to his native country, Nicaragua, to visit his elderly, dying father. He was supposed to return to the United States on Tuesday of the same week he died. How could his promising life be taken from him in such a sudden tragic manner? He was so young, vibrant with life, healthy, strong, handsome and humorous. I was not even given a chance to bid him farewell.

At that moment, everyone from the weekend's retreat, including Serafina and Father Thomas, gathered around me as they heard the heartbreaking news. They immediately began praying for Tony's spirit, for his family and particularly for me. I was overwhelmed by God's love for me. I could not have been in a better place to receive such devastating news. Exactly the right people were around me, who knew what to do in such cases. I was saturated with their prayers, love and support. As I mentioned in an earlier chapter, although Tony and I had broken up, we remained very close friends. My heart had never fully released him.

During the months that followed Tony's death, I understood God's unconditional mercy and love for me. I always wondered why things did not work out between us. In August 2001, Tony and I went out to dinner for his birthday. After a long discussion, he asked me to marry him. To Tony's devastation, I declined. We both cried together. I could not explain to him why I was turning him down. Something within my heart blocked me from accepting. I prayed to God asking Him for an explanation. I never got a clear response from God until Tony's death. The Lord knew the precise second that Tony's life was going to terminate on earth. The Lord was saving my heart the additional pain I would have suffered if I would have agreed to recommit to a relationship with him. The causes behind our initial break-up turned out to be blessings in disguise.

To ease the grieving process, I spent hours daily with our Lord in silent prayer. Meanwhile, the call to return to Medjugorje was still active. My final sign about Medjugorje came in March of 2002. I was praying alone after daily Mass in the Cathedral. Suddenly a man I had never spoken to before, walked up to me as I was prayerfully kneeling. He interrupted my prayer. He said he had something to tell me. He informed me that he had worked as a security guard at the Northern California Medjugorje Conference two years prior in Sacramento. One of the Medjugorje visionaries, who had been invited to the conference, gifted him with several blessed medals from Medjugorje. He told me that he had given away most of the medals except for one. He had kept it for a year not knowing to whom he should give it. He asked the Blessed Virgin Mary to show him who this medal belonged to. As he started giving me the medal, tears poured down from my eyes. I truly felt so unworthy, so small, so humbled. The Blessed Virgin Mary was speaking to me through many people with such clear signs.

In late April, I was suddenly awakened in the middle of the night with Medjugorje consuming my mind. I could not return to sleep. I felt a burning desire to revisit. I logged onto my computer to write to the Prayer Group leaders asking them if there was any room left on the annual Prayer Group pilgrimage in June. To my surprise, they responded positively. Immediately, I decided to charge the trip to my credit card. My reservation was confirmed within a couple of days. In fact, I ended up returning to Medjugorje accompanied by the same three close friends with whom I had been meeting at the cathedral to pray following the events of September 11, 2001. Wendy and Lourdes had never been there before but had heard me talk often about Medjugorje and decided to go with me.

When our pilgrimage bus finally drove into the village of Medjugorje on June 3, 2002, I felt like a little child arriving at Disneyland for the first time. As our bus pulled into the main street facing St. James Church, tears flowed down my cheeks. I was returning to my spiritual sanctuary. My twelve-year old dream finally became a reality. Many things looked different there, new shops, new restaurants, new boarding houses and even a few motels. Nonetheless, the celestial feeling of peace and love embracing the small village of Medjugorje lingered in an almost tangible way.

This trip was distinctly different from my first trip, but equally valuable. I did not witness any miracles; I was not looking for any. I returned to Medjugorje with a different purpose. I was hoping to obtain clarity on the nature of the "call" I had felt over the previous twelve years. I falsely assumed that the Blessed Virgin Mary was going to give me clear answers just like she had done with the signs I received over the previous months. I was wrong. Instead, she wanted to teach me some valuable lessons. I learned that the purpose of Medjugorje did not revolve around a "feeling" of peace. It was not merely an escape from the real world I lived in. Medjugorje was a school to teach me about God's love for us. It also taught me the ways to remain connected to that love. The Blessed Virgin Mary was calling me to live *daily* the Medjugorje messages, not just there, but also back in California. She did not want me to merely talk about Medjugorje. She was asking me to live it, following the villagers' example.

For many years, the local villagers had been faithfully living her messages wholeheartedly. I was amazed how much they gave of themselves to the pilgrims who were there. I experienced that firsthand through many separate incidents. Many gave without any expectations in return. The love of God radiated through them, through their actions and their gestures. God's love was contagious, spreading easily among all the pilgrims. Moreover, there was a sense of unity between everyone, despite the diverse nationalities, languages and ethnicities. I honestly felt a pure love for everyone around me, as if we were all one big family. There were no language barriers. The international language of God was spoken there; that was the language of love. For once, I truly saw us humans stripped of our earthly dividing masks that we wore to disguise our true identities while on earth. I saw us for who we really were: God's precious children.

My experience in Medjugorje reaffirmed to me that the key to maintain this feeling of love was to fully open my heart to God. I needed to *let go* and let God in by surrendering my will to Him. The Blessed Virgin Mary's messages to the world, through the visionaries, were very basic, yet difficult to apply in our secular world. Through her messages, it became clear to me that I was made of both a physical body and a soul. I needed to take care of my soul exactly like I took care of my body. She was asking me to pray with my heart every single day. She wanted my soul to always be connected to

God's heart. How could I know God intimately if I did not talk to him daily, throughout my day? I needed to become familiar with His voice and His guidance. She was asking me to know God more intimately by reading His love letter to us, the Holy Bible. She invited me to make a commitment to attend daily Mass to receive her Son Jesus in the Eucharist. The Eucharist is my spiritual food that nourishes my eternal soul. Just like I eat daily to nourish my body and survive physically, I need to receive the Eucharist daily to nourish and strengthen my soul.

In addition, she was asking me to try to fast on bread and water every Wednesday and Friday. Fasting is not intended to be a punishment; it liberates us from our worldly attachments by taming the needs of our flesh. Are you coincidentally wondering what I meant by *taming our flesh*? I believe our souls came to earth to have a *human* experience through our physical bodies - the flesh. Our spirit must dominate the flesh; otherwise, we lose our spiritual peace and balance. Fasting has immense spiritual rewards; it disciplines the body and strengthens the soul. Even Jesus fasted for forty days to strengthen His soul before He commenced His three-year ministry. The Blessed Virgin Mary often repeats to the visionaries that we can even stop wars if we pray and fast.

Finally, she was asking me to confess my sins frequently, at least monthly. Just like I showered daily to keep my physical body clean and healthy to avoid illness, she was asking me also to keep my eternal soul clean and healthy - to clearly hear the voice of God within my heart and to avoid spiritual sickness that often led to physical ailments.

I realized that these elements were my ingredients for the ultimate attainment of "divine" happiness in this world. While worldly happiness is often short-lived, empty or shallow because it is dependent on the initial excitement of obtaining worldly things, divine happiness does not fade away. I understood that by living the messages that the Blessed Virgin Mary was calling me to live, I was not sacrificing anything, although our secular world perceived it as such. It was quite the contrary. She was giving me the keys to living heaven while still on earth! This confirmed our Lord Jesus' words to us when He said *"...I came so that they might have life and have it more abundantly."*[27]

What a tremendous gift that I was finally able to comprehend, not merely with my mind, but particularly with my heart. I understood what Jesus meant when he said: *"...For behold, the kingdom of God is among you."*[28] The key to inner-peace and contentment was never outside of me. I stopped trying to figure out what my call was. I had total trust in my heart that our Lord would guide me at the appropriate time and place, when I was ready. My task was to work on the daily conversion of my heart. The Lord Jesus must be the center of my life *always*.

---

[27] John 10: 10
[28] Luke 17:21

Chapter Twelve

MY LIFE'S CALL

"He came to Nazareth, where he had grown up, and went according to his custom into the synagogue on the Sabbath day. He stood up to read and was handed a scroll of the prophet Isaiah. He unrolled the scroll and found the passage where it was written:
'The Spirit of the Lord is upon me, because he has anointed me to bring glad tidings to the poor. He has sent me to proclaim liberty to captives and recovery of sight to the blind, to let the oppressed go free, and to proclaim a year acceptable to the Lord.' Rolling up the scroll, he handed it back to the attendant and sat down, and the eyes of all in the synagogue looked intently at him. He said to them, 'Today this scriptures' passage is fulfilled in your hearing'."
- Luke 4:16-22

I returned to California determined to change my life. I resolved to live daily the Medjugorje messages. I knew that our Lord would give me the desired graces as I journeyed further on my spiritual path. My first step was to make prayer as normal to me as breathing. I needed to involve the Lord in every aspect of my life, no matter how trivial it seemed. I desired the Lord to become my best friend, the one I consulted with for everything.

My first step was to make Mass an essential part of my day. I knew that all Catholic churches held daily Masses either in the mornings, at noon or in the evenings. I obtained the schedule of all the parishes throughout the local diocese. I realized that I could attend Mass at most hours of the day. I had absolutely no excuse to ever miss it. I was able to locate St. Mary's Church which was close to my work. I started participating in daily Mass before commencing my work. It felt so wonderful to start my day in prayer and to unite myself to Jesus through receiving the Eucharist. He filled me with inner-peace.

I started seeing the same familiar faces in church every morning. As always, the Lord was teaching me through the people He brought into my life. One particular person taught me an incredible lesson; his name was Bob who was in his late seventies then. He usually sat toward the front of the church while I sat toward the back. I had to pass by his pew daily after receiving the Eucharist. Without fail, I gave Bob a big smile as I passed him. This daily practice continued for a couple of months. One day after Mass, Bob walked up to me to introduce himself. He then told me something very simple that had a powerful impact on my life. He shared with me that he was a recent widow. He was enduring much grief because of the great loss of his wife Antonietta of many years. He told me that every morning he looked forward to seeing my cheerful smile. My smile gave him the strength to endure the rest of his day. I was extremely moved by his words. I thanked him with a big embrace. After he left, I sat in the church pew moved to tears by his words. Something as trivial as my smile was a source of strength to a grieving person. Bob and I have become very good friends since this experience.[29]

The Lord spoke to me so powerfully through Bob. He is always speaking to us, if we pay attention. Sometimes God speaks directly to our hearts; often He speaks to us through other people who enter our lives; many times He speaks to us through nature or the physical world surrounding us. Through my experience with Bob, I learned that every act of pure love produces precious effects in this world. Unfortunately, we do not always see the fruits of a simple smile we might give, a kind word we might say, or a random act of kindness we might perform. Often in life, a simple random act of love is life-giving to someone in need.

A couple of weeks after my return from Medjugorje, I was invited by *PAHIES* - the youth and young adults prayer group that I was involved in - to give my testimony. An invitation was extended to the community at Immaculate Conception Church during Sunday's Spanish Mass. I was initially quite nervous; this was the first time someone asked me to share my testimony publicly about Medjugorje.

When the day arrived, I prayed and asked the Holy Spirit to guide me and fill me. As I shared my story with the forty people who attended, I felt complete love and peace. The hour went by quickly. Many people approached me after the talk to ask questions or to give me feedback. One particular young woman, around seventeen years old, caught my attention. I felt the Holy Spirit asking me to pay close attention to her. When she approached me, she asked me for the website address to obtain more

---

[29] Since this book has been written, Bob has *graduated* into eternal life on August 12, 2008 at the age of 83. He is dearly missed by his family and friends.

information on Medjugorje. As I wrote the address down, I was prompted to ask her how she was feeling. Despite her outward physical beauty and smile, I could sense her shattered heart and soul. She hesitated to answer. She then told me I had many people waiting to speak with me and her story was too long. The Holy Spirit once again prompted me to pull her aside and to speak with her. The Lord was very concerned for this young woman's heart. I followed the prompting and spoke with her outside of the meeting room. As we spoke, she began sobbing. She did not know where to start her story. She told me she had been extremely depressed. In fact, that evening, she was contemplating suicide. She had attempted suicide before but failed. That night her determination was great. Something within her urged her to come and listen to my testimony prior to harming herself. She told me that as she listened to my testimony, she suddenly started feeling God's tremendous love for her through my words. Not knowing why, she felt the need to approach me after my talk.

I was extremely touched by this young woman. I thanked her for her courage to open her heart to me. I began praying for her, asking the Lord to heal and restore her broken heart. We talked and prayed for over an hour. By the end of our conversation, this young woman looked and felt completely different. Her face was glowing with light. The Lord loved and healed her as the night progressed. She left feeling happy and peaceful. I felt humbled by how the Lord used me that night. Despite my broken and sinful humanity, He used me as His vessel to transmit His life-giving and healing love to a young, suicidal woman. He never ceases to amaze me. I went home that night loving Him even more.

One month after my talk at the *PAHIES* prayer group, I was driving on my way to the city of Marysville to attend the Northern California Hispanic Charismatic Youth Conference. My friend Wendy, after her return from Medjugorje, became a very active organizer in the Hispanic Catholic Charismatic Renewal. That morning, she called my mobile telephone to urgently ask me to replace a speaker who had canceled. I was only a few minutes away from the conference. I immediately became very distressed as Wendy was speaking to me. Fears instantly consumed me. I told Wendy I was not a professional speaker. I was unqualified to speak in front of a large group of youth without any preparation. I declined and ended the conversation very upset with her. After I hung up the phone, I felt terrible. I heard the Lord telling me in my heart that Wendy was His instrument in extending the invitation to me. It was wrong of me to behave in such a fearful, unloving manner with her. He reminded me how I had given Him my life and assured me He would give me the words to speak to the youth. I needed to rely on Him and not on myself. I immediately called Wendy back to apologize. I told her I would fill-in for the speaker who had canceled.

I spent the morning in prayer before Jesus, in the Blessed Sacrament. At noon, I gave my testimony in Spanish to over 500 young people. Through my words, the Lord showered the youth with His immensely healing, merciful love. After my talk, many of them approached me to privately discuss their personal pain and childhood wounds. Our Lord was reaching their hearts through me. I felt so blessed to be used as His humble instrument. I received much love from Him as I shared His love with others. It is very true, the more we share His love, the more love He returns to our hearts.

As a result of the youth conference, I was invited in November to speak again at an adult Hispanic Charismatic Conference. There were approximately one thousand people in attendance. The Lord reached the hearts of the adults in the same manner He reached the youth. His love was unconditional and overflowing to everyone willing to open their hearts.

As I was getting invitations from different prayer groups throughout the year to give my testimony, the Lord also planted in my heart a strong desire to deepen my knowledge of my faith. I began reading the Bible regularly. I also read many books about the lives of the saints, the Catechism of the Catholic Church and the Sacraments. I traveled many weekends to educational conferences. I was growing spiritually in ways beyond my expectations. My life became completely centered on the Lord Jesus. I started a prayer group in my apartment on Wednesday evenings. I rarely ever missed daily Mass. I went to frequent confessions, at least twice a month, if not weekly. I tried my hardest to fast on Wednesdays, Fridays, and also whenever I was invited to speak. I wanted to make sure I was doing my best to remain a clean vessel for the Lord's usage.

The Lord was teaching me through all the circumstances of my daily life, especially when I least expected it. One late evening, I had to fly to Chicago for a conference. I was extremely exhausted and hoped to sleep on the flight. When I reached my seat on the plane, I noticed a young mother sitting next to me with a very small child in her arms. The child appeared six months old. Although I loved children, my first reaction was negative. I dreaded having a three-hour flight sitting next to a screaming child. I wanted to rest. To my surprise, as soon as the plane took off, the child fell asleep in his mother's arms. For the next three hours, our flight was extremely bumpy as air turbulences were continuous. I was feeling scared thinking the plane might not make it to Chicago. Many other passengers seemed anxious also. Suddenly, I looked over to the child next to me. He was *still* gently and fearlessly sleeping in his mother's arms, in total trust. At that instant, I felt the Lord speaking directly to my heart. He was teaching me I needed to be exactly like this child in my relationship with Him! No matter how rough or bumpy my life became, I needed to fully trust Him, resting assured He would protect me gently in His arms. I felt so humbled at that moment. Unbeknownst to this sleeping child, the Lord taught me a valuable lesson of trust and surrender. I felt so grateful to have been sitting next to him.

Meanwhile, I became very involved in the *PAHIES* prayer group. I was invited monthly to teach on different topics related to the Holy Bible or our Catholic faith. As I was teaching the youth, I was also educating myself. I spent hours reading in preparation for each talk. The group members became like my second family, my younger brothers and sisters. Some even felt like my spiritual children. I loved each one of them dearly. They confided in me their emotional problems, as they discussed many painful events in their lives. I was so thankful I had learned the lay ministry prayer techniques. I used the techniques as we prayed together for many hours, especially before the Blessed Sacrament.

Through these young people, I have learned about the various things for which today's youth are hungry. They are starving for fatherly and motherly love. Many have never experienced a father's or a mother's embrace. Many ache to hear the words *"I love you my son"* or *"I love you my daughter."* These precious young people are often misunderstood in today's world. The society shuts them out, labeling many of them as "at-risk." The reality is that they are only seeking to be loved unconditionally. Many sought "love" in the wrong places because they never received it in their homes. The false love they received (or the lack of love) was too painful and wounding. It came in the form of physical, emotional, verbal, and very often sexual abuse. These young people sought a sense of belonging and acceptance. I witnessed the Lord set many of them free from their bondage and the lies they had believed about themselves as He renewed their minds. I was so thankful to see the lives of these young people dramatically change through the Lord's love. Some became leaders in the group. Many started living the messages of Medjugorje although they had never been there.

As I look back, I see how instrumental the *PAHIES* prayer group was in my own life. The Lord used it to train and to prepare me for my life's mission. I am eternally grateful to each of the wonderful members of the *PAHIES* prayer group. They have been my true extended family for many years, a priceless gift from God.

In April 2003, I was invited, by someone who heard me speak at one of the conferences in California, to participate in another conference in the State of Guanajuato, Mexico. I was asked to give a talk on a specific topic related to the Catholic faith on the first day, and then to share my Medjugorje testimony on the following day. Sharing my testimony came easily to me. I needed to prepare diligently for the talk I was asked to give on the first conference day. To support me, my close friend Lourdes kindly decided to accompany me on my trip. She reminded me Jesus always sent his disciples two by two.[30] She felt the Lord guided her to accompany me despite the travel expenses.

We were scheduled to depart Sacramento early Friday morning and to arrive at our destination in Mexico around 5:00 P.M. on the same day. Everything seemed to go wrong that day. Our original flight was delayed in another state due to weather problems. Later we were told we had to be re-routed through an unscheduled city. We did not arrive in Mexico until 7:00 am on Saturday morning. We had had no sleep at all. I was so thankful Lourdes had accompanied me. She supported me in handling all the obstacles we faced along the trip.

I was scheduled to speak at 10:00 am. Our host picked us up and we proceeded directly to the house to shower and change. When we arrived at the conference, the organizers informed me there was an unexpected change of plans. One of the other invited speakers, a priest who was scheduled to speak in the afternoon, had had a personal emergency and he needed to depart that morning. I was informed I would replace his afternoon talk. There was a certain sequential order to the scheduled topics; therefore, we needed to switch topics. I could not believe my ears. As I was about to enter into a panic-attack, it dawned on me the Lord was teaching me a very important lesson. He did not want me to give a talk *I* planned. He wanted to ensure it was *Him* who spoke through me. I needed to trust Him by surrendering completely to the Holy Spirit's guidance. I was extremely tired as I had not slept but I decided I needed to completely immerse myself in prayer and fasting until my talk that afternoon. I went before the Blessed Sacrament and

---

[30] Mark 6:7

surrendered my day and myself to our Lord. I felt Him assuring me He would give me the words to speak that afternoon. I just needed to trust Him.

At 4:00 P.M., I was ready to go on the stage. I felt complete peace within my heart. As they handed me the microphone, it suddenly stopped functioning. They handed me another microphone. That also malfunctioned. I could not help but smile. I knew the devil had been working diligently to sabotage my entire trip – the flight delays, lack of sleep and even the last minute change of topics. At that moment, two microphones abruptly stopped functioning. As the audience waited for me to obtain the third microphone which eventually worked, I started joyfully praising the Lord. I knew beyond a doubt that if the devil was being that active, he was afraid of something. I realized instantly that the Lord was going to manifest Himself powerfully through my talk. This empowered me even more.

At once, all my fatigue and exhaustion lifted. The Holy Spirit's strength consumed me. I was in awe at how the Lord worked through me during that hour. The words I spoke did not come from my mind. As I opened my mouth to speak, the words effortlessly came to me. My Spanish was flawless. His loving words were flowing through me to the hundreds of people in the stadium. I knew I was merely a vessel for Him. After I finished my talk I was in complete awe at what the Lord had just accomplished through me. My friend Lourdes ran to me and we hugged each other, crying with joy. We both witnessed the Lord working so marvelously through my complete surrender to Him. The Lord Jesus' words were fulfilled in my life that day: "...*do not worry about how or what your defense will be or about what you are to say. For the Holy Spirit will teach you at the moment what you should say.* "[31]

I traveled back to Medjugorje in June 2003, June 2004 and March 2005. Each year, the Blessed Virgin Mary invited me for a different spiritual purpose, traveling with a different group of people. Each year, several friends from Sacramento accompanied me. Although each trip was equally important, my trip in 2004 was significantly special. I had the great privilege to spend eight days hosted by one of the visionaries, Ivan Dragicevic and his family. He is one of the three visionaries who is still having a daily apparition by the Blessed Virgin Mary. She appears to him every evening at 6:40 P.M. in the chapel in his home. Just to clarify, the pilgrimage was open to anyone interested in attending, and not to specific people. We were a group of twenty-six people from all over the United States. I was so impressed by Ivan's humility and great sense of humor. Throughout the week, I felt blessed by his warmth, genuineness and helpful nature.

Every evening, our entire group attended the private apparition with Ivan in the chapel. I felt extremely blessed and grateful to our Lord and our Mother Mary for this great privilege. We met at 6:00 P.M. and prayed the rosary until 6:40 P.M. when the Virgin Mary appeared to Ivan. One evening, I arrived late in the small chapel. Ivan invited me to kneel next to him, shoulder to shoulder, as we all prayed. I felt very nervous at that moment. I was overwhelmed by the thought that our Blessed Mother Mary was going to appear to Ivan a couple of inches away from me. As the hour approached 6:40 P.M., I could sense Ivan go into a deeper level of prayer. Suddenly, he looked upwards in the air. His voice completely disappeared but his lips were

---

[31] Luke 12: 11-12

146

still moving. His eyes were wide open but were barely blinking. He remained in that position for about ten minutes until the apparition ended. We all then recited together the "*Magnificat*" prayer. This prayer is also known as the "Canticle of Mary" which consists of the words that Mary spoke to her relative Elizabeth as stated in the Gospel of Luke.[32]

After several moments of quiet time, Ivan shared with us what transpired with the Blessed Mother Mary. She appeared to him with a couple of baby angels at her side. He described to us her physical appearance. She looked around 20 years old. She appeared standing on a cloud. She was wearing a long grayish dress blending into the cloud. The dress had long sleeves covering her arms. On her head, she wore a long white veil that covered her head, shoulders and back. She had blue eyes and black hair. She had a crown of twelve golden stars around her head. She was extremely beautiful. Her beauty surpassed anything we had ever seen on earth. She spoke with him in the same way he spoke to us. During the apparition, he completely lost sense of all of the people gathered around him. He could only see and hear the Blessed Virgin Mary. He went into a complete state of "ecstasy." He spoke with a normal voice to her, although we could not hear him. He told us that after they talked and prayed, the Blessed Mother prayed over all of us in the room, giving us her maternal blessings.

During the apparition, I was unable to see the Blessed Virgin Mary as Ivan did. The spiritual veil was not lifted from my own eyes to enable me to see her. I felt with my heart a supernatural presence in the room. I felt an incredible sense of warmth and peace within me. I knew beyond a shadow of a doubt this apparition was authentic, although I could not see what he was

---

[32] Luke 1:46-55

seeing. At that moment, I understood more deeply the reality of the spiritual world around us. It is as real as the air we breathe. We cannot physically see the air but it is essential for our existence. Depending on the temperature, we can sense it in different ways. Sometimes it feels cold, other times it feels warm. Similarly, the spiritual world is invisible but we are surrounded by it. Sometimes we feel its warmth, as when we experience the Holy Spirit or the angels around us. Other times, we experience the cold chilling effects of it, particularly when we experience demonic spirits. We cannot see the angels or the demons, but we definitely sense their presence.

Another noteworthy event occurred during that pilgrimage. One night, I was leaving the church with my friends around 10 P.M. An older Croatian man approached me to speak with me. He asked me if I spoke Arabic. I was surprised by his question as I had never met him before. He then spoke to me in classical Arabic. He told me he was from Medjugorje. He called himself Antonio. He was learning Arabic from all the Lebanese pilgrims who traveled there. He was very fond of the culture. He then disclosed to me private things related to my life and my calling. He assured me the Virgin Mary was always watching over me. He asked me to trust in her maternal love and not worry about anything, no matter how difficult my life became. He then added I would always remain linked to Medjugorje and its graces. He asked for my phone number and e-mail address to stay connected. Surprisingly, on the night I departed from Medjugorje, he gifted me with two pictures to take back with me to the United States, one was of Our Blessed Mother Mary and one was of St. Anthony of Padua. As you might recall from an earlier chapter, the Australian woman that my friends and I met back in 1990 specifically told me to learn more about the life of St. Anthony as it would provide me with powerful lessons for my own life. This definitely was not a pure coincidence. Our Lord never ceases to amaze me. He is always communicating with us, if not directly, then through other people. On a later trip in 2005, I met Antonio's wife and children.

Ever since I returned from this pilgrimage in June 2004, I have been receiving a daily phone call from Antonio every morning around 9:40 A.M. (which is 6:40 P.M. Medjugorje time). This is the time of the daily apparition. He instructed me via e-mail not to answer the phone. The objective of his call is to connect me daily to Medjugorje during apparition time. I am amazed he has been faithfully calling me every day since June of 2004. His daily telephone calls are additional signs of God's immense love for me. Antonio does not ask for anything in return. His actions are pure acts of love prompted by God. I feel so blessed and grateful for him and his wonderful family!

Chapter Thirteen

Taking the Leap of Faith into the Unknown

"Consider it all joy, my brothers, when you encounter various trials,
for you know that the testing of your faith produces perseverance. And
let perseverance be perfect, so that you may be perfect, so that you
may be perfect and complete, lacking in nothing...Blessed is the man
who perseveres in temptation, for when he has been proved he will
receive the crown of life that he promised to those who love him."

- James 1: 2-6, 12

Upon my return to the United States in June 2004, I was inundated with unexpected financial problems. I had recurring mechanical problems with my car, requiring large sums of money to repair and I noticed I was reaching my maximum limit on all my credit cards. When I moved out on my own, I had used my cards to furnish my apartment. I also used them to travel to Medjugorje and to attend the various educational and inner-healing conferences. I never had a savings account as my entire income was used to pay my monthly student loan payments and apartment expenses. I noticed that although I was making payments on my loans over the previous seven years, my balance looked almost the same. Most of my monthly payments applied toward interest. At that time, I had paid around $60,000 in interest alone. This figure is much higher now.

I was still employed in the same corporation where I had started in 1998 holding the same position. I had received annual raises over the six-year period but I felt I was severely underpaid. In 2004, I was still earning 25% less than the person I replaced back in 1998!

I conducted a thorough market salary survey and presented it to my supervisor, the president of the company. I explained how the survey indicated I was earning significantly below the market. I also informed him that after six years of employment, I was still earning significantly less than the person I had replaced. My supervisor stated he disagreed with the surveys as he believed they were inaccurate. He added that he had consulted with his contracted law firm. My salary was within the firm's range for lawyers with my years of experience.

I was shocked by the illogical response. First of all, I was not employed by a law firm. Secondly, I was not employed with the title of an "attorney." I could not understand why he had to contact a law firm to determine my compensation. He did not hold this standard for any other employee within his company. Many employees holding less essential positions earned six-figure incomes with only a high school diploma. I was earning less than that myself despite my various crucial duties and my professional education. I asked him to compensate me according to my current position and all my responsibilities. He informed me that although he was very pleased with my work performance, I had reached my limit on my salary increases. He advised me that if I thought I could earn a better salary somewhere else, the door was open for me to follow that path. I left his office feeling devastated and humiliated. I wished I could resign right away. I felt extremely bitter and angry that my hands were tied by my student loans. I felt so enslaved by them. I did not have the courage, or sufficient faith, to resign without finding another source of income first.

In August 2004, my monthly expenses exceeded my income. This was the first time in my life I could not pay all my bills. I always took pride in how punctual I was in making my payments. I was very organized and completed everything in a timely fashion. Suddenly, I felt like my life was out of my control. I was overwhelmed by my debts. Ironically, two months earlier, I had reached a spiritual peak in Medjugorje. Now, I felt I had plunged financially to the bottom of the pit. I prayed many hours, asking the Lord for guidance. I asked Him to forgive me if I had abused my credit cards in any way. I had used them to finance my spiritual trips and not on worldly things. I saw no rapid solution to my financial misfortune. I spoke to a bankruptcy lawyer in September 2004. He informed me that I was qualified to file a Chapter Seven bankruptcy. He warned me that bankruptcy would only discharge my credit cards and not my student loans. Student loans could never be discharged, except through death.

I went home feeling extremely depressed. I did not know what to do. I felt like I had plunged, once again, into a very deep, dark hole. Despite my faith in God, I felt like I was suffocating. I was overwhelmed by negative thoughts about myself. My situation triggered many of my unhealed childhood wounds and shame. I felt like a complete failure. How could I declare bankruptcy? Much social and personal shame was attached to that. I could not see anything positive about my personal life. I sank more deeply into depression and despair. I was aware and grateful that the Lord had used me powerfully to evangelize and show His love for His other children but at that moment, I needed to see rewards for my hard work in my *own* personal life. Unfortunately, I was so focused on my misery that I deteriorated into deeper darkness. Every night for a whole week, I cried myself to sleep. I was in such deep agony.

One particular night, I stayed awake until 1:30 A.M. I could not sleep. I knelt down in my living-room in prayer. I told the Lord I was exhausted. I had worked extremely hard all my life but had nothing to show for it. I begged Him to explain to me why I did not deserve to see any financial fruits for any of my hard work. I was not trying to be greedy; I was not asking for too much, I just wanted to be financially free from my student loans. I was not asking for a fancy house or an expensive car. How was it possible that I was about to declare bankruptcy and still owe $92,000 in student loans? Where was the "fresh start" I was supposed to obtain through bankruptcy? I felt so expended, so tired of struggling in this world. I wept intensely as the thoughts in my mind tortured me. I finally begged the Lord to transfer my aunt's cancer to me. I had an aunt (my mother's sister) who had been suffering from cancer for the previous three years. She had four children who still needed her. She deserved to live longer to enjoy them and her grandchildren. I was single and nobody depended on me. I believed that nobody would be affected by my death if He took me instead. I felt really spent and ready to move on to eternal life. I could not see any purpose for me in life but to suffer.

Suddenly, I heard an inner-voice asking me to check my e-mail. I thought I was hallucinating as it was very late at night. I had already checked my e-mail at midnight and had no messages. The voice repeated the same command. I finally gathered enough strength to drag myself to my computer. Surprisingly, I saw an e-mail that had just arrived from another aunt who lived in Jordan. Auntie Fifi is also my mother's sister. Due to the time difference, it was already morning there. As I read my aunt's e-mail, I sobbed even harder. She was writing to inquire about my emotional status. She stated she had been feeling great sadness for me over the past days as she could perceive the sadness of my own heart. The Holy Spirit prompted her to pray for me during that week. She did not know what was going on in my life but she was writing to assure herself that I was well.

I was completely astonished with the content of the e-mail. How did my aunt know? Why did she write to me precisely at that hour of my despair? Did the Lord prompt her to send me that e-mail? It would have been impossible for it to be a pure coincidence. I had not spoken to my aunts for several months. There was no way for her to know what I was going through. Nobody knew about my situation, not even my immediate family as I kept things mostly to myself and did not want to concern anyone.

At once, I telephoned her. She was surprised I was calling at such a late hour in the United States. I asked her why she had sent the e-mail. She repeated what she had written. She had been feeling that I had great sadness within my heart. She felt the urgent need to write and inquire about my status. She then calmly said to me the following life-giving words:

"Samia, I do not know why, but I need to remind you of the dream I had of your mother, my sister, when she was pregnant with you. I saw her standing up in the dream. Then, a lovely white pigeon came and stood upon her head. At that moment, I heard a voice saying in Arabic, 'whoever will be born, will be blessed by the Holy

Spirit.' After that, my dear sister delivered her baby and it was you! Remember Samia, you are now in a situation in your life very similar to a woman who is in labor. She endures very deep and excruciating pain. She does not understand why she has to suffer so much. Her time has not come yet to deliver her baby. She needs to patiently wait, trusting in God's precise time. Once the baby is delivered, all her pain lifts quickly as she holds her new baby in her arms. You too, Samia, are in a similar situation. You cannot understand why you are suffering so much. You do not see the purpose as your time has not yet come. Once the time is ripe and you are ready, you will understand the reason behind everything you have suffered in your life."

I could not believe the words I heard her utter. I knew the Lord was speaking directly to me through my aunt. It was impossible for her to have known what I was going through in my life. She lived thousands of miles away on a different continent. Her words directly responded to the prayer I had just made to the Lord right before I checked my e-mail. I could not fathom the incredible love and care the Lord demonstrated to me in one of my darkest moments. He was asking me to just trust Him. There was a purpose for all my sufferings. It was not yet time for whatever was awaiting me. Instantly, our Lord's peace and hope filled me.

At the end of September 2004, I filed for bankruptcy. Even though my ego was completely crushed, I felt as if a great weight had been lifted from my back. All my credit card debts were discharged. I was left with my student loans and car payments. I felt devastated that my credit would be ruined for up to ten years but I had no other option to resolve my situation.

In January 2005, one of my friends was considering switching his career to become a realtor. The real estate market was still thriving then. He signed up to take the appropriate real estate classes to obtain his license. I was encouraged by his motivation and decided to join him for the evening class. I wanted to earn a supplemental income over the weekends to pay off my student loans faster. I paid too much in interest alone. I became obsessed with the desire to pay them off. I often fantasized about having the number "zero" on my balance.

Due to personal circumstances, my friend never showed for the class and I ended up taking the class alone. As a lawyer, I was qualified to apply for the broker's license. I took the test at the end of March and passed. Two months later, my friend Wendy referred my first client to me. I immediately joined a local real estate company on a part-time basis, as an "independent contractor." My close friend Maribel worked there and strongly recommended the company. I was grateful to Maribel's wonderful assistance with my first transaction. A few months after I had obtained my license, the real estate market dramatically declined. It was unbelievable to me. I could not help but wonder if I jinxed the entire real estate market with my negative financial aura.

In October 2005, I took a loan officer class to expand my knowledge of the lending process. Our instructor invited a guest speaker to teach us how to better manage our personal finances. Although the class lasted two hours, it had a dramatic effect on my life. The speaker showed us on a spreadsheet how to payoff all our debts in a specific period of time. The method required strict financial discipline and sacrifices. As he explained his method, I began to see the possibility of paying off my loans in a significantly shorter period than the thirty-year schedule I was on. In order for me to accomplish that, I needed to cut my monthly expenses *significantly*. My only method of accomplishing that was to live in a place free of charge. This would allow me to pay off my loans in less than three years!

The only place I could think of where I could live rent-free was my parent's house. The idea of moving back was not easy as I would lose much of my independence. I had changed significantly since the last time I lived there in March 2001. I was more spiritually developed and more emotionally healed. I knew my return to my parent's house would not only help me with my finances but also would enable me to enjoy my parents as they aged. Their life is a gift. They have been an essential part of my journey and I thank the Lord every day for their lives.

During that month, I spent many hours in silent prayer every single day. My days always started with Mass. In addition, after work every night I went to the chapel to spend time with Jesus. I spent three to four hours in Adoration of the Blessed Sacrament. To truly know someone in life, we have to spend time talking to them, as often as possible. My desire to know Jesus on a deeper level grew greater every day. One night while in prayer, I asked Jesus why He did not talk to me as much as I talked to Him. I knew He was real and alive, even though I could not physically see Him as His apostles did, I firmly believed in Jesus' Real Presence in the Blessed Sacrament.

In the hope of not digressing too much from my story, I am convinced God talks to *all* of us in our hearts, if we listen in silence. That is what prayer is all about. It is a sincere, intimate conversation with God. We talk, He listens. He talks, we listen. Our spirits are connected to Him all the time. We are used to being surrounded by loud noises, televisions, radios, CD players,

DVDs and iPods. We have become so accustomed to noise that, often, silence frightens us; it might force us to look within ourselves. We must be in solitude to connect to God. He speaks to us in the silence of our hearts. A very dear person to me once challenged me when I said to him that the Lord spoke to my heart. He said to me these unforgettable words: *"Who do you think you are, for Jesus to speak to you? Do you think you are the chosen one? How do you know that Jesus is the one who is speaking?"*

Frankly, you might also be having similar thoughts as you read these paragraphs. If you are, I can empathize with you. For many years in my life, I also thought that God only spoke to chosen people, such as prophets or religious leaders. I believed He would not speak to somebody like me. Since I commenced my inner-healing journey, my thinking has changed because the Lord has been healing my heart and renewing my mind. I've started to believe in who I truly am. I am a daughter of God! I might not be the chosen one, nevertheless, I cannot think of a bigger joy than to be His daughter. That is great news for you too.

You are His precious daughter or son too!

You might be wondering how I know that Jesus *is* the one speaking to me. When Jesus speaks, His voice *always* brings my heart much peace and love. He sounds very gentle and meek. The more time I spend with Him alone in prayer, the more His voice becomes familiar to me. This is true of any conversation I have with my friends. The more frequently I talk to a friend, the easier it is for me to recognize his or her voice. The same is true with our Lord. His enemy usually speaks to our minds and not to our hearts. Unlike the Lord's voice, the devil's voice is very condemning, deceptive and lacks all love or humility. His words are destructive and often filled with hatred. Even if the devil tries to disguise his voice as that of God's, he would get exposed rapidly if we as God's children have a close relationship with God through prayer. The devil cannot be humble or loving. He is filled with pride. It is hard for him to disguise himself for too long.

Allow me to pose some very simple questions: *Are you a parent? Do you have any children? If yes, do you love them? How often do you talk to them? Can you see yourself going for days, weeks or even years without ever speaking to them, especially when you know they are suffering or in need of you?*

Well, our relationship with God works the exact same way. The difference between God and our earthly parents is that God is PERFECT. He is all LOVE. He does not have a wounded heart filled with false beliefs and lies as we do. He could never hurt us or abandon us. Our relationship with our own parents is not so flawless. Most likely, much of our heart's wounds resulted from the dynamics of our childhood, particularly our family environment and our relationship with each of our parents. Most of the time, we project onto God many things we have experienced with our own parents. For example, if we grew up with an unloving, mean, merciless father, most likely we would project that onto God, the Heavenly Father. If our father was physically, emotionally or sexually abusive or had abandoned us, we would most likely believe that our Heavenly Father is equally abusive and would abandon us also. This behavior usually results in our harboring much anger and resentment against God.

Our parents could only "love" us in the way they best knew how to love. They tried to raise us in the only way they knew how, based on their own woundedness and background. Despite that, they still communicated with us regularly, sometimes more than we desired. God also tries to communicate with us in multiple ways: directly to our hearts, through others, through nature, through music and songs, through events in our lives and even through the material world around us. I believe His favorite method of communication is to speak directly to us through our hearts. We cannot hear Him if we are not listening.

In case you are wondering, when I use the word "heart," I am not referring to the actual muscular organ in our body that pumps blood to keep us alive. I am referring to the innermost part of us, our soul. I believe that our soul *is* the heart of our spirit. The purpose of our soul is very similar to our physical heart. It helps maintain the vibrant life within our spirit. It is the place that contains all our *true* and intimate feelings, our desires and where we are real and authentic. Our soul also encompasses our free will and our conscience which guides us to know the difference between good and evil.

Whenever we are truly connected to our hearts, we should be able to experience God's presence within us. He speaks directly to us from within, not from the outside. The problem arises when we are too afraid to connect to our hearts. Many believe it is too painful to *feel*. Many have had such heartbreaking experiences in life that "feeling" becomes an unpleasant event. They learn to do everything possible to numb the feeling or the pain. The secular world cheerfully offers us plenty of ways to do that, to self-medicate and escape our pain and kill our feelings. Ask any alcoholic or drug addict why they *truly* abuse their addictive substance? Of course, many will respond immediately *"because I like it. I like how it feels. It gets me in a better mood."*

I have been given that answer by many people, including close friends. After we sit and have an intimate, honest conversation, the truth always comes out almost the same *"I drink because it is too painful; it hurts too much to feel the pain. I need to forget. Alcohol (or it could be drugs, food, work, gambling, sex or pornography) helps me forget."*

Through my experience in life, I have become convinced that all these things that society labels as a problem (such as drug-addiction, alcoholism, sex addictions, pornography, food addiction, gambling and overworking) are merely symptoms. They are all substitutes to numb our pain, to forget, to change our moods and to avoid our true feelings. The core cause of the pain *is* the real problem. Most likely, the cause is something that originates from infancy or early childhood wounds. Maybe we never bonded to our father or mother; as a result, we seek to bond to "someone" or even "something" to replace that emptiness or to cover up the resulting shame. Maybe our father or mother walked out on us when we were children. As a result, we are filled with shame, believing we are unworthy, unlovable, guilty, responsible, or a mistake. Toxic shame *is* the root of most addictions. In addition, we might have experienced a family environment filled with violence, physical, emotional or sexual abuse.

Having the ability to feel is a gift from God. *Feelings* are true blessings. When we *feel*, we connect to our soul, to our spirit's heart. That is where we find God and connect to Him. When we avoid *feeling*, we disconnect from the source that connects us to God. That is precisely the reason the devil's primary objective is to disconnect us from our feelings and fill all our minds with lies. The lies are so common to us that we have stopped seeing how blatantly false they are. I will demonstrate. Let me know if any of these statements sounds familiar.

"It is too painful to feel. Why would you want to do that?"

"If you feel the pain, you might not be able to handle it. It might kill you."

"It was your fault to begin with. Don't think about it; try not to feel it."

"Just forget about it. Go out, get drunk, smoke some weed to relax, maybe even snort some cocaine. You will feel much better after that. I promise you!"

"Just stuff away your emotions with food even if you just ate. Don't worry about it; it just makes you feel better. You're not alone. Food is your best friend."

"Are you crazy? You think God will help you. Where was He when you were suffering? He totally abandoned you. Just forget about Him. You don't deserve His love. Let's go out partying and forget everything."

"God will never forgive you for what you have done. It does not matter how much pain you were in when you did it. You are worthless. It was all your fault. Just give up. Drink it away. You'll feel much better afterwards."

The list goes on and on. Did you relate to any of it? Do you think I am completely off? I respect your opinion. It is a product of your own life's experience. You may disagree with me. I am only speaking from my experience.

God talks to all of us if we connect to Him with our hearts and cleanse them through His healing love. The cleaner the heart, the better is our reception of God. Two of the biggest blocks that prevent us from hearing God are anger and lack of forgiveness. We often hold on to them because we

162

are too afraid to let them go! Again, we believe all the different lies the demons delightedly inject in us, such as: *If I forgive or let go of my anger, then justice will not be served; I might get hurt again; If I hold on to unforgiveness and anger, then I can punish the person who hurt me.*

As I have mentioned in an earlier chapter, unforgiveness and anger hurt only *us*. We poison ourselves when we keep them within us. They are very toxic to our souls. They keep us in bondage, attached to the enemy, the devil, and disconnected from God's love that is attempting to reach us. I recommend that you get rid of these negative emotions in the safest way you know how. For myself, I usually ask God to give me the graces I need to forgive. Often it is hard to forgive on our own because the pain is too great. God has unlimited graces to give us. Please ask for them. I promise you He will give you what you need. He loves you! I know it is hard to trust, especially after being hurt. As infants or children, "trust" is the first thing we lose when we are hurt by someone who is supposed to love and protect us. You have to allow God to come into your heart to help you heal all the pain. Surrender the anger to Him. He will gladly remove it. He cannot come into your heart if *you* lock the door. He only knocks gently. Will you please open? I know I did. He has healed many things within me. He still continues to cleanse my heart daily. It is a lifetime process, one day at a time. The process is part of our journey and that is why it takes so long sometimes. Most often, the lessons are learned *through* the healing process, not afterwards.

Going back to my story, I had been spending several hours alone with our Lord everyday. I asked Him why He was quiet most of the time. I knew I was rather talkative. He seemed overly quiet. Suddenly, I heard an inner-voice in my soul gently command repeatedly: "*Be still.*"

It took me over thirty minutes to shut off my brain and focus completely on my heart, my inner soul. When everything felt extremely quiet within me, I started hearing Him speak to me, clearly. His voice sounded like my own inner voice. I knew the voice was not my own. The thoughts He shared with me were too wise to come from me. Jesus revealed many things to me about my life. One thing He emphasized was the importance of being patient in life. Patience was a crucial ingredient of faith, trust and surrender. It was crucial for me to learn how to be patient, if I were to go to the next level spiritually. Jesus stressed that He had never abandoned me. He was more united to me than ever, especially through my suffering and hardships. He was grateful for my perseverance. He thanked me for trusting in His love enough to have gone to Him with my anger and despair.

He showed me how He always sent me help when I needed it. Every person who walked into my life played a part of His plan for my being. Every situation I endured contributed to my own spiritual growth and benefit. Instead of focusing on the negative aspect of the situation, He asked me to focus on the lesson to be learned. With every situation in life, I needed to ask one simple question: *What am I supposed to learn from this?* Even when terrible things happened to me, which were not parts of His plan for me, Jesus asked me to surrender them to Him. Jesus explained that many dreadful things happened to us in life that He would not stop, not because He was powerless, but because He gave all human beings "free will" which He would not violate. He reminded me of St. Paul's words: "*We know that all things work for good for those who love God, who are called according to his purpose.*"[33] Even when bad things happen to us because of someone else's abuse of their free will, God could always bring goodness out of the situation, if we give it back to Him.

His words filled my heart with His peace. I felt peaceful about my decision to move back to my parents' house. No matter how difficult the situation would get, I needed to remember that there was a lesson for me to learn there.

The Lord taught me another powerful lesson several days later. I was in the chapel around 9 P.M. All the other people left by 9:15 P.M. and I was planning on staying there to pray until midnight. I started praying the rosary prayer. Around 9:30 P.M., I heard police car sirens outside of the chapel. At first, I was not concerned but the siren noises increased and were accompanied by the sound of one or two helicopters circling the area. The chapel I was praying in was located in what is commonly known as a "rough" part of Sacramento. As I heard the sirens, I became frightened. The sounds seemed too close. I stopped praying. I wanted to go outside to see what was happening. As I was about to get up to look outside, I heard the Lord's voice telling me gently: *"Samia, why are you afraid? Are you not here with Me? I will protect you. Be at peace and continue your prayers."* I gazed at the Blessed Sacrament which was exposed in front of me. I knew it was Jesus, but, at the moment, my faith became shaken. I needed to see Jesus in the flesh! I slipped out of the pew, excusing myself from our Lord, to see what was happening outside. I opened the door and saw the street filled with eight to ten police cars while two helicopters in the sky were circling the area. I looked in the church's large parking lot and saw my small car in

---

[33] Romans 8:28

complete solitude. Nobody was in the chapel area except me. I locked the door immediately and rushed back into the chapel. Once again, I heard the Lord's voice asking me: *"Samia, what do you fear? Why do you doubt? You are with Me, your God. I am Omnipotent. Trust and continue your prayers. I promise you everything will be fine by the time you need to leave at midnight."*

I know this might be hard for you to believe. I was *still* afraid, despite what the Lord was telling me. I am amazed by how weak my human nature can get sometimes. I picked up my mobile phone to call my friend Wendy. I wanted her to turn on her television or radio to see if there was a news-flash on what was happening outside of the chapel. I knew it had to be serious. I was afraid that the suspect might try to break into the chapel or even into my car to hide. I could not reach Wendy. Finally, I knelt down in prayer and tried to refocus. I asked the Lord for forgiveness for my weak faith. I attempted to pray in the midst of all the sirens outside. The noise was constant for approximately two hours and fifteen minutes, until 11:45 P.M. By then, I had managed to shut off the noise and had gone into deep prayer. When I looked at my watch, I realized it was completely quiet outside. I was in disbelief. I slipped out of the pew once again to see what was happening outside. I looked out and discovered that the street was completely empty, no police cars, no noise and no helicopters in the sky - just my lonely car. I returned to the chapel in tears. I knew the Lord was about to teach me something powerful. I sat in silence and waited. Jesus spoke to my heart the following words:

"My child, this is to teach you that no matter how many sirens are going around you, whether in your own personal life, or in the physical world

around you, just keep your eyes fixed on Me! Do NOT fear anything. Focus your eyes on Me always. I will get you through all the situations and provide you with all the protection you need."

I left the chapel, having learned a priceless lesson I will never forget. I often wondered if the situation outside of the chapel was real. I knew what I saw and heard. One thing I can assure you, I have endured various "sirens" in my personal life since then. I knew exactly what to do and it worked!

I spoke to my parents that week about moving in with them. They were very pleased with my plan especially since my sister Sophie had left for college one month earlier. They were already experiencing the emptiness from her departure. I gave my one-month notice to my apartment manager and packed everything in my apartment for storage. On November 25, 2005, I moved back to my parents' house. As of August 2007, I am still living there, awaiting the Lord's next step for me.

During the first few months, I was able to pay off my car completely from the rent money I was saving. I also paid off the two smaller student loans. I was left with $80,000 to pay. From that perspective, things were looking very positive for me.

Nevertheless, the situation at my employment was getting worse. In December, I was anxiously waiting to be paid an annual bonus that I had become accustomed to receive. Although it was a small amount, I counted on receiving it to help me make a bigger loan payment in December. To my complete surprise, my supervisor did not issue me a bonus that year. I found out from other managers that they received theirs. When I negotiated my salary with my supervisor back in 2004, he promised me the bonus as part of my annual compensation. I was so upset and hurt that I cried for an hour.

I could not fathom what my supervisor had against me personally. I felt he treated me as less valuable than the other employees. I consistently excelled in my work performance. My duties had increased significantly over the eight years. I was wearing three different hats in the company. In addition to my regular title, I also became the corporation's officer for two distinctly separate government regulatory compliance requirements. I never complained about the ludicrous volume of work in my department or that I had no clerical support. My work was very sensitive in nature; one small regulatory detail I might overlook could cost the corporation thousands of dollars in state penalties. There were never any complaints against me from anyone who worked with me. In fact, I was very well-liked by everyone in the company and our business associates.

At that point, I started resenting myself for not having the courage to resign. What was wrong with *me* to accept the situation instead of walking away? The choice was completely mine. I could not blame my supervisor for my own lack of response. In general, my supervisor was a very good humble man. I considered him as a good friend with whom I shared much laughter and many good discussions. I had nothing against him personally. After all, he was also God's precious child, my spiritual brother. He was generous with most of the other employees. I was the only one he seemed to treat differently, for a reason unknown to me. I often wondered if he had something personal against lawyers.

I prayed very hard to our Lord about my work situation. The Lord clearly told me in my heart that I needed to resign. Of course, I was looking for an easier answer from the Lord. Didn't He know I needed another income first? I asked the Lord to help me find other employment. I did not have the courage, or the solid faith, to resign without another assured income. The rapidly declining real estate market was commission-based, without any health benefits. I could not rely on that.

In February 2006, a full-time manager, whose responsibilities affected the contracts I was in charge of, resigned. I was very sad to see him leave as he was an outstanding employee who worked with much diligence and heart. Nobody was hired to replace him, but one day, I was called into my supervisor's office. He instructed me to temporarily assume the duties of this manager. I wanted to scream when I heard that. As you recall, I had previously *temporarily* managed two departments for over nine months, working insane hours. I was not willing to go through that again, especially when I felt that my supervisor did not seem to appreciate my dedicated work. I told my supervisor I was already extremely busy and that, as this was a department very different than mine, it required a full-time person to manage it. My supervisor responded that there was little work to perform in the other department and it would only occupy a couple of hours out of my day. I was shocked by his response. I knew my supervisor's statement was not accurate. The position required much hard work, supervision of employees, extensive traveling and organization. I knew it was not a part-time position.

I anxiously awaited my therapy group day in April. Once I verbalized my condition, I began to connect with all the feelings burning within my heart. All the buried anger suddenly surfaced. I never imagined I was able to hide so much anger within me. It was secretly poisoning me. After processing my anger, I got in touch with all the injustice I felt within me. I felt ashamed of myself for taking the abuse for so long. I also felt ashamed that I did not value or love myself enough to walk away from the situation. I felt ashamed of all the fears I had. The group members supported my desire to speak directly with my supervisor or to resign. It was clear to everyone how much injustice and lack of appreciation I endured at my job. It was up to me to make a stand for myself.

During the following week, I attempted to contact my supervisor a couple of times regarding my overwhelming tasks. The department I assumed required me to travel to give training in a distant city on Wednesday. I also needed to finish working on the proposal that was due on Thursday. I could not physically be in two places at the same time. I worked past midnight every night. I never received a response from my supervisor instructing me how to prioritize my tasks. I felt so unsupported and disrespected. After several sleepless nights, I completed the proposal and submitted it by the deadline.

On that Friday, I called in sick. I was mentally drained and emotionally devastated. It happened to be "Good Friday." This was the day Christians commemorated the crucifixion of the Lord Jesus. I went to church that afternoon to pray. On that specific day, I wholeheartedly connected with Jesus' suffering and passion for me. As He was crucified for us, I felt like I was being crucified with Him. I wept for His suffering and my own.

I stayed praying in the church for many hours. I asked the Lord to speak to me about what I needed to do. He spoke to my heart so clearly that day. He compared my work situation to that of victims of domestic violence. The victims stayed in the relationship year after year hoping it would improve. The victims were consumed with fears of the unknown. They accepted the abusive situation since it was familiar. They were too afraid to walk away. They were afraid they would not find another spouse to replace the abusive one. They were too afraid to remain alone or not to have their daily needs met. Ultimately, they decided to stay until another partner came along to save them from their misery.

The Lord showed me I was doing the exact same thing. I worked in this company for a total of eight years. From the beginning, I knew I was underpaid, but I stayed in my job, hoping that if I worked hard my employer would eventually recognize my worth and would compensate me appropriately. I was filled with fears. I could not venture outside of my safe environment as I got accustomed to the work I did. I was too afraid to resign. What if I did not find other employment quickly? What if I remained unemployed? What if I could not pay all my monthly bills? I had stayed there hoping to find another position to walk into so that I could resign.

The Lord also taught me that before I could effectively represent someone else as a lawyer, I first had to be able to stand up for myself. I needed to love and value myself first before I could genuinely love others. He asked me to surrender completely to Him in total trust. He reminded me of the child I had seen years earlier asleep in his mother's arms on the plane. Nothing disturbed him no matter how rough the ride became. He was asking me to do the same thing. He told me He would provide for my daily needs. I was His precious daughter. He would never abandon me. He knew me better than I could ever know myself. He was asking me to take the biggest leap of faith in my life into the total unknown. He reminded me of His words for us when He stated: "...*seek first the kingdom [of God] and his righteousness, and all these things will be given you besides. Do not worry about tomorrow; tomorrow will take care of itself."[34]*

For the next two days, I fasted and remained in prayer. I wanted to ensure that whatever decision I reached was in total union with God's Will for my life. Sunday happened to be Easter day. I felt so much peace in my heart as I celebrated the resurrection of our Lord and His victory over death.

I sat down and wrote a four-page resignation letter. I wrote it all in one sitting. I felt the Holy Spirit prompting each word I wrote, each fact I listed. I wrote everything in this letter I wanted my supervisor to know, everything I wished to tell him in person. I was resigning without giving the company any prior notice. This was not a practice I would have ever done under normal circumstances. I always thought I would give at least one month notice prior to any resignation. I felt after being so disrespected and devalued, resigning without notice was the only option I had. I knew beyond a shadow of a doubt I was doing the right thing for my dignity and for myself.

Monday, April 17, 2006, became *my* resurrection day. I arrived at work early in the morning. I painfully wept as I quietly gathered all my personal belongings in my office. Even though I knew I made the right decision, sadness and grief tore like daggers right through my heart. I was leaving a whole family behind; I really loved *everyone* with whom I worked at the company. For over eight years, we had laughed and cried together; we had celebrated so many happy occasions together. I planned to walk away in silence without saying any farewells. It was *extremely* painful for me to do that. I was afraid if I told anyone I was resigning, a chaos might have occurred at work. I thought the best decision was to quietly submit my

---

[34] Matthew 6:33-34

resignation letter, turn in my keys, and walk-away silently, allowing everyone their normal workday. I drove away from the building that day knowing that my life would never be the same.

This was the first time in my life that I had stood up for myself when the consequences appeared to be dire and extremely painful. It was the first time I ever had the courage to defend myself.

This was the first day in my life I truly began to love myself!

Chapter Fourteen

The Merits of My Life's Difficulties

"...whatever gains I had, these I have come to consider a loss because of Christ. More than that, I even consider everything as a loss because of the supreme good of knowing Christ Jesus my Lord. For his sake I have accepted the loss of all things and I consider them so much rubbish, that I may gain Christ and be found in him."

- Philippians 3: 7-8

I was thirty-six years old, living at my parents' house, unemployed, and financially broke. Ironically, I felt liberated and peaceful! I experienced complete freedom for the first time in my life. The Lord had stripped from me everything material upon which I had previously relied. It was a very humbling but *painful* process to teach me detachment from my worldly securities.

First, the Lord took away my personal freedom and privacy. He did that when He prompted me to move out of my apartment into my parents' house in order for me to pay off my student loans more quickly.

Secondly, the Lord detached me from my financial independence. He allowed my circumstances at work to become so intolerable that I had no choice but to resign. I did not have any other stable source of income. I needed to rely on Him to fulfill my daily needs.

Thirdly, the Lord disposed of my dependence on my reputation. I had a prestigious position at the corporation. I was very well-liked by everyone with whom I worked. It felt great to be loved and esteemed by others around me. The Lord showed me I needed to detach myself from seeking the world's affirmation or approval. It would always disappoint me as it was imperfect and often self-seeking. He wished me to seek always His love and consolation as He would never disappoint me or abandon me.

Finally, He stripped me from my "self" or ego. He detached me from the worldly seduction attached to the "attorney" title. According to the various law firms I applied to, I was not qualified for anything. From the law firms' perspective, I had wasted nine years working for a corporation instead of a law firm. I needed to start over from scratch, the same level as a first-year lawyer. I had worked in a corporation setting for over eight years and did not have the traditional "attorney" position. There was absolutely no value placed on my work experience or my skills. In fact, one legal recruiter advised me to limit my search for employment to corporations. I followed his advice but to no avail.

Despite all my external losses, I felt much inner freedom and peace. I had nothing to worry about! I had forgotten what that felt like. The only payments I had to make were my student loans. Even if I did not make them, the lenders could not place me in jail. I could defer most of them as long as I had no income. My credit was already ruined by my bankruptcy, so I did not have to worry about my FICO credit score either. When a person hits rock bottom in life, it is extremely liberating. One wise priest once told me during confession: *"Remember this always: when you are down to nothing, God is up to something!"* God bless this priest! He was absolutely right.

Thankfully, I had my real estate license to fall back on to support myself. The real estate industry did not discriminate against me and warmly welcomed me in! Here comes the ironic part. With each real estate transaction I closed, I took home more money than I did working a full-month at the corporation. I worked fewer hours, was my own boss, had more tax-deductible income, and worked with clients who truly appreciated my help. Each client I represented felt like family. One client jokingly offered to rent me one of the bedrooms in his family's new home after we closed the purchase transaction. The Lord brought me one transaction at a time. During the periods I had no transactions, He brought me legal work which I performed on a contract basis. There were a few instances when my legal education brought me financial rewards. The Lord always provided me with sufficient money to pay my bills, nothing extra, just the right amount. He was teaching me He literally meant what He said when He taught us in the Lord's Prayer "give us *this day* our daily bread." He was teaching me to depend on Him *daily* for each need I had. I had no business worrying about tomorrow. That was His concern, not mine.

Through prayer, the Lord helped me to see my entire situation differently. My mind was getting repeatedly attacked by negative thoughts about myself. I know now these thoughts did not come from my mind but from the demonic spirits around me, who sounded exactly *like* my mind or thoughts. The voice tortured me repeatedly with such sentences as the following: *You are a complete failure. You are a mistake in life. You have failed in every way possible. You don't deserve to live. Why don't you just end it all, just take your life, it will be much easier for you. You have no purpose in this world. Can't you see that?*

My loving Lord Jesus persevered in speaking His truth to my heart, setting me free from the enemy's bondage and lies. I once asked the Lord why He had allowed me to work at my previous employment. I felt I had ruined my life by working there. He gently responded that I did not ruin my life by working in that company. He reminded me of my initial reason for becoming a lawyer. I did it because I wanted to *help* people. He reminded me of the tens of people I helped there. They came to me with so many different personal needs. He showed me how the lives of many were significantly changed because of my assistance and love. Consequently, some of these people were enabled to become His significant instruments to help hundreds more. There was a positive ripple effect to everything I did. He asked me to stop judging my life or my success in life through worldly eyes. Not everything we do in life has a monetary compensation. He will reward us in heaven for many things which nobody notices or rewards here on earth. He also told me that my law degree was not a waste of time. There was a purpose for it in my life, as it gave me credibility when I spoke or preached. The Lord was using it for *His* purpose and in *His* own way. I was "practicing law" in a *spiritual* manner. All the hardships served their purpose for my spiritual growth and especially pulled me as close as possible to His heart, to a full union with Him. I need Him every day, every minute and every second. He *is* my lifeline. Maybe if I had obtained a position in a large law firm, earning a lucrative salary, I would not have had the time to allow the Lord to heal my own heart or enable me to help others. So often in life, we get lured by money and prestige so we frequently sell our souls and compromise our own inner-peace and contentment. It was through my own inner-healing journey that I learned to forgive the people who hurt me and, more importantly, to forgive myself. I now learned to have tremendous compassion for myself, when I used to be my worst self-critic. As a result, I am able to have real compassion and love for others. The secular world could have tempted me with its material rewards, if I had been spiritually weak. God *always* knows what is best for me.

Of course, through worldly eyes, I appeared as a complete failure, a *loser*. Although I was thirty-six years old, I had nothing material attached to my name, except huge student loans and a fairly new car that broke down on a monthly basis. I had no husband, no children, no house, no pets, no sports utility vehicle, no boat but also no migraines! I was peaceful and stress-free. I cherish the wisdom of Mother Teresa of Calcutta - a Catholic nun familiar to many of us – who often taught: *"God does not demand that I be successful. God demands that I be faithful."*[35]

Sadly, we live in a superficial world which values humans by their external, material attachments. What kind of car does one drive? How many square feet in one's house? What brand names does one wear? How many carats is the diamond he gave her? The latter is something I do not quite comprehend even as a woman. Perhaps I am just an odd woman. Many women, all around the world, seem to define their *own* value – or the value of their relationship with their future husbands - by the carat weight of the diamond on their finger, instead of the *sacred union* of their two equal souls. The larger the size of the carat weight, the more treasured or "loved" she

---

[35]Gonzalez-Balado, Jose Luis. *Mother Teresa in My Own Words.* Gramercy Books, 1996, 40.

perceives herself to be. If the carat weight is too small, she wonders what her friends in society might think of her or her future spouse. When are we going to wake up to learn that the true priceless diamond is *not* the one that is placed on the finger, but is the one to whom the finger belongs!

Regardless of your gender, *you* are that unique diamond with the perfect cut and size. We do not need anything outside of ourselves to define our value. Our worth is completely priceless. We were born and created with it. It is already *within* each of us. We do not need to do anything to earn it or prove it. Don't you know who you truly *are*?

You are God's precious child!

Regardless of religion or creed, we are worth every drop of blood Jesus shed for each of us individually because He deemed it so. He died for each equally, whether we are aware of that now on earth, or will only realize it later in heaven.

Going back to my story, exactly one month after my resignation, I suddenly developed a deep desire within my heart to write a book. At first, I thought I would write about all the *rape* (sexual abuse, sexual molestation and incest) of infants and children occurring in this world. As you recall, I had been praying privately with many people for their inner-healing. I also had frequent invitations to speak in many conferences and prayer groups. In addition to sharing my Medjugorje experience, I was being invited to preach about God's love, mercy and healing power. After my talks, many people always approached me to privately discuss their life. They trusted me as they felt God's love through me when I spoke. The majority of the people, regardless of their gender, age, or nationality, repeatedly shared the same childhood trauma with me. The majority of these males and females had been *raped* as children or infants. The numbers far exceeded what people could fathom. It was the leading horrific crime that most people were too ashamed to discuss or to disclose publicly. The innocent victims were consumed with shame, guilt, self-blame and many lies about themselves, especially their sexuality. These atrocious crimes occurred and recurred in silence. I greatly admire public television figures who openly disclose their sexual abuse. Finally, someone has the courage to break the toxic silence and to release their lethal feelings of shame. We cannot deal with a problem if we remain in denial about it. We must tackle it head on.

I received my first confirmation about my book on June 16, 2006. I went out to lunch with a very dear friend of mine, Kristin. I enjoyed spending time with her as I felt her amazing connection to God. I perceived that about her the first day we met. She had a beautiful presence that I recognized immediately. God's love clearly emanated through Kristin's soul and body. Despite the differences in our backgrounds and beliefs, we connected on a very deep spiritual level. Kristin was raised LDS which is the Church of Jesus Christ of Latter-Day Saints. We enjoy discussing our numerous spiritual experiences in life.

On that day, somehow the subject of Medjugorje came up as I was talking about the first time I ever experienced God's love in my heart. Kristin was not familiar with my Catholic faith, so I tried to explain in greater depth what was transpiring in Medjugorje when I went there. Suddenly, Kristin turned to me and said these memorable words: *"Samia, you have to write a book about your life. It cannot be just for Catholics. It has to be for everyone!"*

I felt the Lord speak to me directly through Kristin that day. She had no idea I had been getting prompted by God to write a book. Kristin insisted my book had to be about my life and not the subject of sexual abuse. She felt I had a story that needed to be shared with the world. I thanked Kristin for her encouraging words and support. I told her I would be praying about our discussion.

When I arrived at church that same afternoon to attend daily Mass and pray, I saw one of my dearest friends, Ana. In many ways, Ana was very similar to Kristin. Her beautiful joyful face always radiated God's love. I could not help but smile whenever I was in her presence. Her cheerfulness was contagious. If you'd ever meet her, you would also agree! Ana was one of the coordinators of the *PAHIES* prayer group and I usually saw her in daily Mass. I shared with Ana what had transpired with Kristin. Immediately, Ana confirmed to me that Kristin was right. Ana believed that what Kristin told me was a clear sign from God, especially since Kristin was not Catholic. Ana believed that I was not employed in a full-time position to enable me to write a book.

Two days passed since my meeting with Kristin and Ana. I was getting ready to go to Mass on Father's Day. I was praying to our Lord to guide me about the book. Suddenly, as I looked into my mirror, the title of the book flashed before my eyes: *"The Bridge between the East and West."* I knew these words were not coming from my mind. I immediately knew in my heart that I had to write a book about my life. The bridge represented my life as I journeyed from Jordan in the East, to the United States in the West. My whole life had been a journey toward discovering God, even when I was not consciously aware of it. I had so many astounding things happen to me throughout my life. My journey has been filled with so many faith-strengthening experiences that manifest God's love. For the sake of brevity, I recounted only some of them in this book. With each incident, I saw God's love reflected in the details of my life. He wanted me to know Him on an intimate level. With each experience of my life, particularly the painful ones, He pulled me a little bit closer to His Heart. Ironically, it is usually through difficult times that we open our hearts to God. Maybe we do it out of despair, maybe even out of anger or fear. Regardless of our reasons, the Lord always welcomes us back into His loving and open arms.

Over the course of the months that followed my conversations with Kristin and Ana, I went frequently to the chapel to pray before the exposed Blessed Sacrament. I asked Jesus for clarity. I wanted to ensure that the idea of the book was coming from Him. I was trying to live my life in complete alignment with His divine will and not mine. The Lord spoke clearly to my heart every time.

In June 2006, He asked me to start writing down the specific things He wanted me to remember. He stated:

"Your book is your next step in life. I prompted Kristin and Ana to tell you what they did. Your book will provide you with the answers to your questions and prayers. It will give you an understanding of your entire life thus far. It will only take you thirty days to write if you remain completely united to Me. To accomplish this, you need to continue attending daily Mass, preferably in the mornings. Try to start your day with Me. Confess your sins regularly, weekly if possible. Pray the rosary daily. Spend time with Me daily in Adoration, three hours if you can. Make every effort to fast on bread and water while you are writing. You need to remain a clean vessel. Read often

the Sacred Scriptures. Learn more about Me, My Word and My Life. Slow down and listen! Slow down and listen to Me in every situation. Learn to slow down, always. Let go completely and be patient. Let go of your control. Come to Me with all your needs and troubles. I promise to guide you in every situation. I will give you the peace that your heart needs. Always be humble, loving and obedient in everything. Remain gentle and meek. That is the true sign of strength. Look at how I reacted to Pilate and the Scribes. I faced insults and injury with love. Evil crumbles against humility and love. Remember that always."

I was in awe of the Lord's specific instructions. I no longer needed any confirmations. I just needed to follow His instructions. At that moment, it became clear why my legal employment search was fruitless. I had surrendered my will to the Lord; clearly He had other plans for me. At first, I became very happy and excited about the project. I knew exactly what to do, step by step. I started telling all my friends and family about my intention to write a book. The problem was, I only talked about writing the book. I had a rough outline and even started the first chapter. Every time I contemplated following the Lord's directions, I would instantly be overwhelmed with fears. At first, I thought my fears stemmed from the strange things that suddenly started occurring to me. As I drove my car on the freeway, I often felt the presence of demonic spirits around me trying to harm me. I know this might sound crazy to you, but I would not mention it if it were not true.

To give you an example, I would be driving within the speed limit on the freeway late at night. Often there were few cars around me. All of a sudden I would have a car drive next to me as if it were trying to push me off the freeway or to run me over. At first, I thought it was a pure coincidence.

When it happened frequently, I started to get scared. Furthermore, although I had bought four brand-new tires in August 2006 and had a two-year old car battery, I had three flat tires and a dead battery within a three-month period. Even, my car's windshield was getting hit by many rocks that were flying into it. At first, I did not think much of it. I had six major rocks smash my windshield during one week. In all of my life, I had rarely had a rock hit my car. During that week my windshield was so damaged, I had to replace it. Currently I have a new windshield that is less than one-year old with new rock cracks in it. I am just leaving the newest rock crack as a souvenir. I cannot afford to replace the windshield one more time. On a positive level, the fact that I was being frequently attacked felt like I was on the right path. That is usually when the demonic spirits bother us the most. Demons do not bother us much if we are already off-track or heading in the wrong direction. Even though they were attacking me, the Lord showed me His protective love and power each time. Nothing ever happened to me personally. The Lord always sent me help right away. When bad things occur around me because of demonic interference, I now pray and patiently await angels to help me. Also, the Lord allowed the demons to manifest themselves so clearly to show me how real and present they were. Many people have stopped believing there are demons around us, but they *are* real. I am a witness to that. Despite their reality, we should not be afraid of them. The Lord has already triumphed over them and has given us authority over them. We just need to believe in the power of His name.

My fears indicated that I needed more inner-healing. Thinking about writing this book triggered deep wounds within me, especially my rejection and failure wounds. Over the twelve months after I felt the call to write it, the

Lord allowed certain situations to occur in my life that activated these wounds. Some situations revolved around my living situation. Others revolved around close friends' betrayals and misunderstandings. Regardless of the scenario, the Lord used all my triggers to take me back in prayer to the source and origin of my pain. As I prayed, I felt enclosed in a dark immobile place, understanding it to be the womb, and even there the demons injected their blatant lies. Incident by incident, the Lord liberated me with His healing truth each step of the way. Even my therapist Alysa commented that it was clear that the Lord had me on a fast-track for healing.

When Alysa was not available, my friend Lourdes, a prayer minister, often prayed with me. The healing process was difficult. I was in so much emotional pain that I wept regularly. The fact that I did not have a full-time job with specific hours, allowed me to work on the healing of my heart while enabling me to spend much time in prayer. Not only did I attend daily Mass, I often attended Mass up to three times per day – morning, noon and evening - in different churches throughout the Sacramento Diocese! You might be judging this as excessive or abnormal behavior but I relied on the Lord's graces and strength to persevere through every minute and second of my day. I felt the need to unite with Him Eucharistically as often as possible. During that period of time, I received the biggest inner-healings of my life. These healings were crucial for me to be able to produce this book. As you recall from my childhood experience, I was so afraid to speak out about my life. I was filled with lies about what could happen to me as a result. All the cultural wounds and lies I carried from my childhood in Jordan resurfaced. I tackled the lies, shame and pain one at a time. It was not easy but the Lord finally set me free with His Truth and Love. It took me over one year to finally be able to commit to the thirty days the Lord was asking of me.

I was so thankful to our Lord that He placed many people in my life to help me as the journey got tougher and tougher. I was very close friends with Father Thomas, the priest I mentioned earlier, who was part of Joshua Ministries. As a hermit, Father Thomas lived mostly a life of solitude and prayer. He had become my emergency hotline for intercessory prayer. I called him regularly to pray for me. He often celebrated Mass for my specific intention and for my protection. He administered some of the Catholic Sacraments[36] to me when he visited Sacramento. I cannot thank our Lord enough for giving me such a special gift through Father Thomas' life and ministry. I am grateful for the way the Lord continuously manifests His love through all the people He places around me.

Writing this book became a collaboration of love! Numerous people were used by God as His obedient instruments to complete this project. For almost two years, my own parents generously provided me with daily shelter, nourishment and their prayers; living in their house, rent-free was a great blessing since I had one less thing to worry about.

In case you wondered about the image of the lady on the cover of this book, it is a very special picture which I took in Medjugorje. This is the image that was painted of our Blessed Mother Mary according to the description of the Medjugorje visionaries. The original painting hangs in the conference hall of St. James Church. It is *Gospa*'s picture.[37] *"Gospa"* is a

---

[36] Eucharist (Holy Mass), Reconciliation (Confession) and sometimes the Anointing of the Sick (James 5:14-15)

[37] © Informativni centar "Mir" Medjugorje www.medjugorje.hr

Croatian word that means "our Lady." This is one of the many titles Catholics give to our Blessed Mother Mary. Everyone in Medjugorje refers to Mary as *Gospa*.

With respect to the design of the book's cover, the Lord clearly showed me that He had selected my friend Ana, a talented graphic designer, to design the book's cover. He told me He would give her the exact image He wanted on the cover and asked me to trust her discernment. Ana and I both went to Mass and Adoration to pray before she commenced her design. The final product is Ana's outstanding work as inspired by the Holy Spirit. But wonderful to tell, even though I had never previously discussed it with Ana, you can imagine my delight and awe when I referred to my diary of one year prior when our Lord was instructing me to write this book. Skimming through my diary's pages, I discovered I had made notes (under the inspiration of the Holy Spirit) concerning the book's cover about a dove, a bridge, water and a silhouette of our Lady. As you can see, these are the exact components of Ana's final version of the cover.

My friends Kristin, Lourdes and Rasmiya reminded me regularly that I needed to take the time to write the book. They frequently asked me how the writing was going precisely when my fears were blocking me from fully responding to God's call. The Lord was prompting my friends to remind me to stay focused. Even my friend Alvin often prepared me his delicious barbecued ribs so that I could relax and feel his supportive love. My friend Wendy offered me her house so that I could have a quiet place to write. She even organized a team of our friends to pray for me every single day of the thirty days I wrote.[38]

My friend Kristin reviewed and edited the initial chapters of the book as I wrote. My friend Rasmiya reviewed and gave me great feedback on several chapters. Last but not least, our Lord led me to a wonderful pious lady, Mrs. Martha Wilson, a retired educator, to edit the final manuscript of the book prior to sending it to the publisher. Martha is another precious gift from our Lord! I am very thankful for the all unconditional love, support and prayers from my family and friends. I could not have accomplished this task without them. I love each of them dearly.

After I received incredible inner-healings that rid me of much fear, shame and lies about myself, my heart was finally ready to take on the challenge. I started writing my book on precisely July 17, 2007. The Lord promised that I would complete my book in thirty days, if I followed His instructions. This would fall on August 15, 2007. This day "coincidentally" happened to be a very big feast day in the Catholic Church. The Church celebrates the Assumption of the Blessed Virgin Mary into heaven.[39] On that day, Father Bill, a very wonderfully spirited and gifted priest at Immaculate

---

[38] The prayer team included my amazing friends Rosalba, Lourdes, Wendy, Ana, Raul, Vernel, Marizol, Lenneris, Lorelis, Maria, Father Thomas and Mirella. In addition, I also had many other friends who knew me and were praying for me too, such as Kristin, Brooks, Maureen, Maribel, Eduardo, Miguel, Debbie, Bob, David, Celia and Connor. Special thanks to my friend Justin for his insightful contributions to my life.

[39] The Catholic Church has traditionally taught that after the Blessed Virgin Mary completed the course of her earthly life, she was assumed body and soul into Heaven. She was transported into Heaven with her body and soul united.

Conception Church, blessed my book and dedicated it to our Lord Jesus and Blessed Mother Mary.

I just *love* how our Heavenly Father works. Each detail of my life has been so meticulously designed by Him. There have been no coincidences. Every aspect of my life mirrors His great love for me. I am patiently anticipating what He has planned for my life in the years to come as I try to live daily in alignment with His Will. Maybe there will be a sequel to this book as God's Truth and Love continue to unfold throughout the journey of my life. I can only come to one conclusion as I am finishing this book: GOD IS JUST PERFECT.

GOD *IS* LOVE!

Chapter Fifteen

The Enemy of Love

"Then the Lord God said to the serpent: "Because you have done this, you shall be banned from all the animals and from all the wild creatures; on your belly shall you crawl, and dirt shall you eat all the days of your life. I will put enmity between you and the woman, and between your offspring and hers. He will strike at your head while you strike at his heel."

- Genesis 3: 14-15

I have spoken much about the inner-healing aspect of my journey, particularly the lies I believed about myself and how these lies left me in bondage and pain. Have you ever wondered where these lies come from? How do we fall into false belief systems? Regardless of our religion, creed, beliefs, gender, age, nationality, social status or ethnicity, all of us have shared one thing throughout our life's journeys: *suffering.*

Why does God allow this suffering if He loves us? Why is there so much pain and misery in our world? I have pondered these questions for a long time. I am confident that similar questions have also crossed your mind. In the midst of my agonizing pain, particularly through the inner-healing aspect of my journey, and through my prayer ministry to others, the Lord has been gently guiding me to the answers. What I will share with you next is my own interpretation of the answers, based on my life's journey so far. To be safe, let's call them "*Samia's Theory.*" Of course, you do not have to agree with any of my answers or accept them but my thoughts might challenge you and challenge your beliefs. I am grateful that you are allowing me to share my thoughts with you.

To be able to address the questions posed above, we have to start from the *beginning*, not of my book, but of the creation of the world. Jews, Christians and Muslims embrace the first book of the Old Testament, *Genesis*. I also believe that God created the world and the first human beings as described in *Genesis*, chapters one through three. I do believe that the devil is real. His original name was Lucifer. *Lucifer* is a Latin word meaning "light-bearer." As a child, I was taught that Lucifer was a fallen angel, known to us now as Satan. I was also taught that Lucifer was a prominent archangel in heaven, who motivated by pride, rebelled against God. He was cast out of heaven, along with a third of the angels. We refer to these fallen angels as "demons," who were expelled from Heaven. Satan embodies evil and *is* the enemy of God. It is believed that the catalyst that drove Lucifer toward rebellion against God was the creation of humans and the revelation of the incarnation of our Lord Jesus. Lucifer was very prideful as he considered this an insult since he perceived himself as superior to humankind.

The Lord Jesus gave a great description of Satan, the devil. He said:

"...He was a murderer from the beginning and does not stand in truth, because there is no truth in him. When he tells a lie, he speaks in character, because he is a liar and the father of lies."[40]

I know that Jesus always tells the truth. Jesus *is* Truth.[41] First, Jesus confirms to us that the devil *is* real, not a figment of our imagination. He describes him as a "murderer" since the beginning of time. He also describes him as a liar, calling him the "father of lies." It is out of character for Satan to speak any truth. It is against his nature as there is "no truth in him." It is really important for you and me to understand this essential fact and be reminded of it. The devil is such a good liar and he has us so deceived by his lies that he has succeeded in transforming the lies into accepted "truths" in today's world. He is an expert in this field! **His only power is deception**. He attempts to deceive us through the lies he tries to inject into our minds, thus altering our truth into his falsehood. Otherwise, he does *not* have any control over us. **Jesus has conquered and defeated the devil through His death on the cross and His victorious resurrection on the third day**. We just need to keep our eyes fixed on the Lord Jesus and the word of God. Regardless, the devil is still in our world for a purpose and he has only one objective: to destroy our souls by making us believe that God does not exist, and even if He does, He does not love us and has completely abandoned us; therefore, there are no consequences to any of our behavior while on earth and our life's journeys have no ultimate purpose.

Although the devil realizes he has been defeated by Jesus, he knows his only power left is deception. The devil operates today in the exact manner he

---

[40] John 8: 44-45
[41] John 14: 6

has operated since the beginning of Creation. He seeks the destruction of our souls through our cooperation, through the exercise of our own "free will." *Genesis* tells us that from the beginning of Creation, God created Adam and Eve to live in His presence filled with love, peace, and harmony. They were God's intimate friends and had dominion over everything around them. They walked with Him and talked to Him. God generously shared with them all the blessings of His Creation. He gave them something very priceless with which He Himself would not interfere: "free will."

Because of God's omnipotence, it might appear as if He has relinquished part of His power by giving us our free will. This sounds contradictory but God *is, was,* and *will always be* in full control, despite our free will. No matter how the world is around us – whether wonderful or horrible - God *always* has full authority over all of His Creation, including Satan and his demonic spiritual team. Since the beginning of time, God *is* present equally at every moment. God does not abide by what we know as "time" or "space." He is present outside of both. Having said all of this, God tolerates evil because our will chooses the evil over the good.

I believe when God gave us our free will, He did it because he wanted each of us to *choose* Him, but not out of force or obligation. Personally, I can relate to that. I would not find any gratification in forcing a man to love me, in controlling him or manipulating him into loving me. What value would that have? Where is the pleasure in knowing that the man I love has no choice *but* to love me? I would be ecstatic to know that he *chose* to love me, knowing he could have chosen any other woman in the world. I believe that God is the same way. He wants us to *choose* to love Him above all. He will never force us to love or obey Him. He wants to share heaven with all its glories with each one of us. St. Paul tells us: "...*What eye has not seen, and ear has not heard, and what has not entered the human heart, what God has prepared for those who love Him.*" [42]

Satan has known all these things since the beginning of Creation. He does not want any of God's children to share in the glories of God in heaven, our final home. That is precisely why he began his conniving attacks against Adam and Eve. As an expert in lying, he approached Eve to trick and convince her to do exactly what God asked her and Adam *not* to do. God had given them full liberty in the Garden of Eden with the exception of one thing. He asked them not to eat from the Tree of Knowledge of Good and Evil as it would lead to their death. Out of His love for them, God disclosed to them the harmful effects of consuming the fruit of this tree. It was fatally poisonous separating them from God's presence through their death. God wished for them to be obedient but He would not force them. He gave them their free will to *choose* life or death, to *choose* to be physically with Him or separated from Him through death.

Satan made a blatantly exaggerated, untruthful statement to Eve to lure her into his scheme. Even though he knew that God had asked them not to eat from the Tree of Knowledge, he asked her if God had commanded them not to eat from *all* of the trees in the garden. Eve innocently responded, correcting him that it was *only* one tree they could not eat from or they would die. As Satan could not force Eve against her will, he lured her into his scheme precisely the same way he seduces all of us. He made a statement that was clearly false. He said: "...*You certainly will not die! No, God knows well that the moment you eat of it your eyes will be opened and you will be*

---

[42] 1 Corinthians 2:9

like gods who know what is good and what is bad."[43] Although the statement clearly contradicted God's truth, it deceptively made Eve feel that she was *missing out* on something big, as if God was purposefully depriving her of something that was rightfully hers. It is precisely in such moments of strong temptations that God asks us to call on Him for help, for His free divine assistance. He aids us by giving us all the graces we need to resist the temptations. We do that through prayer, by connecting to His heart.

Eve exercised her free will to disobey God by believing the lies. Instead of preventing further injury, she helped Adam disobey God also. Of course, Adam had free will also. Neither one of them attempted to resist the deception or remained obedient to God. It was through their usage of their free will that death entered into the world. *Sin* was an act of disobedience to God's instructions.[44] It was through the human will that sin entered into the world. God did not cause their fall, quite the opposite. He told them exactly what to do to avoid their death. God was not punishing them by allowing them to die. He gave them a clear choice with specific instructions. He did not force them either way and they had to live with the consequences of their choices.

One very essential fact to note is Adam and Eve's reaction after they ate from the tree. We are told in the third chapter of *Genesis* that their eyes were opened and they knew they were naked. They tried to cover themselves. Later, when they heard God walking, they "hid" themselves from Him

---

[43] Genesis 3:4-5

[44] The Catechism of the Catholic Church defines "sin" as: "an offense against God as well as fault against reason, truth and right conscience. Sin is a deliberate thought, word, deed, or omission contrary to the eternal law or God." (1849, 1853, 1854).

because of the *shame* they felt. When God called on them to see where they were, Adam replied and said: "*I heard you in the garden; but I was afraid, because I was naked, so I hid myself.*"[45] God replied to Adam with an interesting question: "*Who told you that you were naked? You have eaten, then, from the tree of which I had forbidden you to eat!*"[46]

It is important to emphasize that there are consequences to our actions. Adam and Eve felt ashamed, afraid and aware of their nakedness. They hid themselves because they were too ashamed to reveal their true, authentic inner selves. Have you noticed how far back Satan injected the poisonous shame into the human mind? He started shortly after Creation, through the cooperation of free will which resulted in disobedience to God and separation from Him. A friend once pointed out to me – and I agreed - that Adam and Eve ingested Satan's wicked shame precisely through self-judgment, as was implied in *Genesis*.[47] Shame is a very dangerous poison that makes us feel defective, inherently flawed, inferior, unworthy and unlovable. The devil and his demons inject shame into our minds directly through our own self-judgment. Shame is also injected into us via other channels that violate the free will which God gave us. This occurs when others around us abuse their own free will by violating ours through their aggression - physical, emotional and sexual. This results in creating deep wounds within our hearts which Satan scornfully stuffs with his shame and lies. Satan and his demonic team

---

[45] Genesis 3:10

[46] Genesis 3:11

[47] This understanding of shame and the roots of our wounds was explained by William Cook in his Master's program thesis entitled "*Yes Father, Forgive Us - A Model for the Integration of Christian Spirituality and Psychotherapy,*" 1994, Trinity College of Graduate Studies, Orange, CA, USA.

are always attacking us, particularly through our minds by their deception in the same way as they treated Adam and Eve. They continue "scratching" our wounds by amplifying our lies about ourselves and others around us. Their primary objective is to fill us with enough shame to make us believe that we are unworthy of God's love and have been abandoned by Him.

Allow me to give you a very common example that, in my opinion, causes the most severe wounds of our hearts. I know this subject might be uncomfortable and might trigger a wound but I feel a sense of urgency to expose the devil's atrocious scheme in our world as it is destroying the lives of millions of infants and children. Many children grow into their adulthood while still suffering severely from the effects of having been molested or raped. As I shared earlier, I was almost physically raped while in Europe. I was certainly violated or raped emotionally and spiritually. I am very grateful to our Heavenly Father for rescuing me from the physical rape. Nevertheless, I suffered the emotional scars and the resulting trauma as my innocence was about to get shattered. I was not a child then but a twenty-year-old woman. The act was *not* my fault. I was clearly an innocent victim of another person's abuse of his free will. I did not cause the situation or desire it. It was a horrific incident completely out of my control so why was I filled with shame, guilt and fear afterwards? Why was I left in bondage and lies? My dignity was certainly violated, not physically, but emotionally. My feelings were very similar to those of Adam and Eve when they first disobeyed God and felt ashamed and therefore they hid. In my situation, I was innocent but in the case of Adam and Eve they felt shame, fear and guilt because they realized they had disobeyed God. Back in 1990 when the incident occurred, I did not discuss it with anyone for twelve years. I managed to block it within my mind and deny the damaging effects which resulted. I hid my inner self also. What was the root cause of my reaction? Where did it come from? Why was it that no matter how much I tried to verbally or mentally tell myself that it was not my fault, I still felt guilty, shameful and unclean? My thoughts did not make any logical sense then.

After receiving prayer ministry about this incident, the Lord Jesus freed me from my lies and healed my wounds with His truth and love. He liberated me from the devil's oppression and removed all the poisonous shame that he had injected into my mind as I internalized his lies. Even though I already knew that I was innocent and without guilt, I could not bring that knowledge to my heart by myself. The lies had been implanted by demonic spirits and could not be removed by a human being. It took Jesus' divine healing love and truth to bring lasting peace to my heart. I learned tremendously from this experience. Despite the horror of the incident, it helped me identify with and help many people who were victims of rape (incest, sexual abuse and molestation) as children. Let us call it for what it truly is: the rape of innocence! Out of shame, our society attempts to reduce and conceal the brutality of this act by calling it "molestation" or "abuse." The Lord Jesus wants me to share with you what I have learned!

Rape is a purely evil act, orchestrated by Satan himself, operating through human free will. Satan's purpose is to destroy the victim's soul, to shatter and violate childhood innocence, and to desecrate by distorting the perception of one of the most beautiful gifts that God Himself shared with us: the sacred act of procreation! It is the sexual act that produces a human life, one of God's precious children. To deface and mutilate the sacredness of this act, Satan launches an attack on the most vulnerable, pure and innocent amongst us, our infants and children. He schemes against them because of their innocence and purity. He knows that if he could destroy innocence by distorting and tarnishing the sacredness of the procreative act and injecting shame and lies about it at such a young age as infancy or childhood, his work with these children would be done for life! As infants and children, we learn things from our surroundings and our first interactions with the world around us. When pure and innocent children are raped, their innocence and first learning experience about their sexuality and the sacred act of procreation gets completely distorted and deformed. This act was *never* meant to be introduced to children at such a vulnerable and innocent age and in such a defiled manner. An extremely sacred and holy act has been transformed by Satan into a source of lethal shame. Victims are then prey to feelings of guilt, rage, secrecy, self-blame, unforgiveness of self or of others, blatant lies and internal confusion about their own sexuality.

I have talked to many male and female adults from all walks of life and cultures who were innocent victims of such horrendous acts. The numbers in *both* genders are very high, especially in the male population. Unfortunately, the shame attached to male rape is even greater than that of a female. Instead of being an advocate for the innocent male victims, society shames them more by bringing their m*asculinity* into question. The lives of both men and women victims were severely affected by these infancy or childhood crimes. The consequences ranged widely; many had intimacy problems as adults, many became sexually promiscuous in their early teens, many became confused about their sexual orientation, many acted out their rape by becoming perpetrators themselves and raping other innocent children and many tried to numb their pain through severe addictions to alcohol, drugs, sex, pornography, food, cigarettes, gambling, shopping or even work and many went into hiding, completely denying the rape in order to be able to survive. The shame and the lies that were internalized were often overwhelming. The devil felt scornfully victorious over God's innocent and pure children! This is such a deplorable crime which occurs repeatedly in our world but many people are too ashamed to look at it or discuss it! Won't more people stand against the continuous silent massacre of innocent and pure souls? Won't more people have the courage to break the silence and permanently rupture the devil's shaming web?

Our Lord is also *outraged* by these crimes against His innocent and pure children. I cannot help but recall His passionate discourse and forceful words against anyone who commits crimes against His innocent children whom He considers to be the greatest in heaven. Jesus revealed it when His disciples asked Him a question:[48]

"At that time the disciples approached Jesus and said, 'Who is the greatest in the kingdom of heaven?' He called a child over, placed it in their midst, and said, 'Amen, I say to you, unless you turn and become like children, you will not enter the kingdom of heaven. Whoever humbles himself like this child is the greatest in the kingdom of heaven. And whoever receives one child such as this in My name receives Me. Whoever causes one of these little ones who believe in me to sin, it would be better for him to have a great millstone hung around his neck and to be drowned in the depths of the sea. Woe to the world because of things that cause sin! Such things must come, but woe to the one through whom they come!"

---

[48] Matthew 18: 1-7

Tragically, most of the rape perpetrators were once rape *victims* themselves!!! I want to make it very clear that I am **not** saying that every rape victim becomes a rape perpetrator. Most do not. However, the majority of the perpetrators were themselves once a victim! I *personally* think most of them were. This is a vicious demonic cycle in which Satan has gained much territory. He set the wheel of innocence-violation in motion for generations and generations. More people must take a stand to break this evil cycle! I want to. What about you?

The Lord Jesus has *never* abandoned any of His precious children. He suffers equally with each victim as the Lord is connected to each one of our souls. As we suffer, He suffers along with us in silence. It has *never* been part of His plan that any of these dreadful things happen to any of us. Despite His omnipotence, He will not interfere with our free will. Rape perpetrators have free will and He will not go against their will. Miraculously, He intervened in my case. It was not because He loved me any more than He loved any of His other children who had been raped. Our heavenly Father just answered my prayer instantly as I trustingly cried out to Him for help, from the depths of my soul. Maybe if my physical rape would have taken place, I would not have had the strength to continue my journey or have had the strength or perspective to write about it today. He demonstrated to me His power and His love as He rescued me physically and later healed my emotional wounds and scars. I am a witness to the power of His healing love. If you happen to be a victim of rape, I want to assure you that His love and truth can heal you! I know that firsthand. He can liberate us from our lies and heal all our wounds. He permitted the horrendous act because He would not interfere with the human will; however, He wants to heal the consequences of it. The Lord Jesus stated that to us when He read the words of the prophet Isaiah that were fulfilled in Him: "*The Spirit of the Lord is upon me, because he has anointed Me to bring glad tidings to the poor. He has sent me to proclaim liberty to captives and recovery of sight to the blind, to let the oppressed go free, and to proclaim a year acceptable to the Lord.*"[49]

Jesus came to bring to *all* of us, regardless of our differences, the good news that He *is* still alive today and is here to liberate us from the bondage of Satan's lies. Jesus wants to restore our "sight"- our physical, emotional and spiritual sight. He wants us to be "free" from our "oppression" which is causing many people in today's world to be severely depressed and filled with despair and hopelessness, depending on one or more anti-depression pills to survive each day.

This is Jesus' time to bring the joy and freedom back to our souls and hearts. He clearly stated "...*I came so that they might have life and have it more abundantly.*"[50] Yes, Jesus wants us to live life in abundance. I do not believe He is referring particularly to "financial" abundance here. Jesus was poor Himself. He never sought money, luxury or fame in His life. Jesus was humble and simple in His ways. He came to give us the *Good News* of love, forgiveness, mercy, healing and freedom. In fact, Jesus healed many physical ailments but also many emotional ones too. I invite you to read closely - on your own - the Gospels of Matthew, Mark, Luke and John and to note something very important. Jesus healed people from "demonic spirits" or an "unclean spirit" throughout these gospels.[51] It was clear that He healed many

---

[49] Luke 4: 18-19
[50] John 10: 10
[51] Matthew 10: 1,8, 12: 22-28, 43-45; Mark 6:7-13, Luke 9: 1-2, 10:17-20 and others.

people physically - the blind, the lepers, the paralytics, the deaf and even the dead. However, many people neglect to see the significance of all the people that Jesus set free from demonic oppression and also demonic possession! He gave that authority to all his twelve apostles and even his seventy-two disciples when He sent them out to evangelize and heal His other children.

An essential part of Jesus' ministry to the world as stated in my quote above is His healing ministry - physically, emotionally and spiritually! Jesus *is* alive today as He was over 2000 years ago. I believe He is present with us everywhere spiritually. I also believe and am fully convinced that he is fully present with us Body, Blood, Soul and Divinity through His Presence in the Eucharist (Blessed Sacrament). I have witnessed with my own eyes the miraculous healings that He has performed and is still performing today! He is truly *alive* and wants to set His children free from the devil's snares, oppression and deception. Are you seeking that freedom? Are you going to let some of your childhood wounds - such as fear, anger, doubt, unworthiness, self-blame, unforgiveness or rejection - get in the way of your soul's freedom?

That is absolutely our choice. We have free will. Like I previously stated, even Jesus will not go against our free will to heal us, He needs *our* surrender and cooperation. Jesus loves us completely. He is Mercy and Love. In His mercy, he forgives all our offenses, sins and transgressions no matter what they are or how grave we judge them to be. This means that no matter what our past has been, if we truly repent, He will forgive us. He tells us *"Behold I make all things new.*[52]*"* If you do not take anything from the

---

[52] Revelations 21:5

lessons in my life's journey so far, I pray that you will at least remember the most important lesson I learned:

Jesus' love and mercy will always be greater than any offense we have done on our life's journey. He loves us so immensely that He died for each one of us, including YOU, yes, YOU. Even if you were the only person alive, He would have still died for YOU on the cross. We are worth it to Him, no matter what our past has been. He knows all the wounds of our hearts and everything we have ever lived through or suffered, all the loneliness, the rejection, the abandonment, the self-blame, the guilt, the tears, the despair, the anger and the abuse – physical, emotional or sexual. He knows all our hearts' intentions and why we did what we did in life. We just need to trust in His love and mercy. He wants us to seek His abundant mercy. He will forgive us. We just need to ask for forgiveness with humility and a repentant heart. He wants us also to forgive ourselves and not be afraid. Jesus has conquered death and defeated the devil! What is there to fear?!

I will end this chapter with a true personal story that demonstrates the strength of our own free will. I had a close friend who suffered a major accident which left him physically handicapped in one leg. The surgeons performed many operations to save his leg and it was saved but did not function properly. Because of this, my friend lost his employment which was physical in nature. He was extremely depressed and filled with anger and despair. His accident affected every aspect of his life. I truly felt my friend's pain and wanted to help him by praying with him for the healing of his emotional and physical wounds. My friend angrily rejected all my offers. He was very angry with God, not just because of his accident but also due to many childhood wounds which left him in severe, emotional pain. Since my friend rejected God and did not seek His healing love, he sought the remedy that the devil gleefully offered. My friend tried to numb his pain through many addictive behaviors. These addictions led to his life spiraling further downward. Out of my love and care for my friend, I prayed for him before the Blessed Sacrament and fasted for nine days. The Lord Jesus showed me that He would heal his leg on one specific day if he would come to the chapel where the exposed Blessed Sacrament was exposed. This would be a proof to my friend that Jesus is alive and loves him. My friend needed to come to Jesus to receive his physical healing. Since I did not dare to contact my friend and mention God to him, I asked God to have someone from my friend's own family contact me on the day the healing was supposed to occur. The Lord Jesus showed me in prayer what would happen if my friend came to Him. Even though I could not prove it, I knew beyond a shadow of a doubt that my friend's leg would be physically healed if he came to the chapel.

On that day, my friend did not call me, however, his mother did. She told me that she suddenly felt a prompting in her heart to contact me. She wanted to make sure I was fine. I recounted the full story to her and told her to bring her son to the chapel as Jesus was going to heal him. I promised her that Jesus would fulfill what He told me. My friend's mother telephoned him and informed him about what I told her. He was very angry when she mentioned God and refused to come. She telephoned him again and told him that I would wait for him in the chapel until midnight. He told his mother that he would think about it. I waited patiently in the chapel and prayed for my friend's heart to soften so that he could come and receive God's healing love for him. I waited until midnight. When my friend did not arrive, I felt great sadness in my heart. I told the Lord Jesus that I could not understand why my friend did not come. How could anyone not want to be healed? I *knew* his leg would be healed that day. I knew that my friend's life would improve significantly as a result. How could he say no to the miraculous healing of his life? The Lord gently told me the following words:

"This is just to show you how powerful is the human will. I will never go against it."

The Lord then explained to me that my friend did not come, purely out of fear. He was scared about the consequences that would have resulted from his healing. If he got healed, he would have had to change his life and his ways. Clearly, my friend allowed his fear and lies to prevail. His fears led him to choose darkness over light, thereby rejecting God's healing love. God does not heal us – physically, emotionally or spiritually – if we do not acknowledge Him. We have to say *YES* to Him first.

I finally asked Jesus if my friend lost his chance to be healed since he did not show up on that precise day. Jesus' astounding response was:

"I AM TIMELESS."

Chapter Sixteen[53]

SCHOOL OF LOVE

"See what love the Father has bestowed on us that we may be called the children of God. Yet so we are. The reason the world does not know us is that it did not know him."

- 1 John 3:1

Our life's journeys are similar to jigsaw puzzles. Each piece in the puzzle has a different cut and place and stimulates our brain to develop and grow. Some pieces are easy to fit in while others are extremely difficult and challenging, but every piece in the puzzle is equally important in producing the final masterpiece.

Similarly, our journeys on earth form the framework for our spiritual education and growth. Every person and event in our life can serve a good purpose.[54] Each fits into our life differently depending on the objective or the lesson to be learned. Each is important in our life, regardless of the type or duration of our relationship. Some people or some events are more challenging to fit into our life than others. It might take us longer to adjust or

---

[53] The author recognizes that Chapter Sixteen includes many metaphors and is not trying to create a new dogma in the Church or create a new theology.

[54] Romans 8:28

to deal with, as they might cause us confusion and pain. Others are very simple and straightforward and each contributes to our earthly journey and spiritual development in one way or another. Every person and event in our journey is essential in completing our education.

The circumstances of the events - good or bad - that create each encounter we have with another human being, become the catalyst for our growth. We are not meant to live in this world alone. Each one of us has a specific role on earth and a unique assignment. We each form a particular piece in someone else's jigsaw puzzle. We all need each other to be able to complete our life's puzzles (*assignments*). None of us are here by accident, whether we were conceived with much love or even perhaps were unplanned. Maybe our parents were not married; perhaps they just happened to meet and shared a brief sexual encounter; maybe we are a product of a violent rape. Despite the specific situation, God has a purpose for the life of each one of us!

He did not cause any of the evils we may have experienced in our lives, but He turns these evil experiences into good in order to achieve His purpose for our lives. We are His children first before we become the children of our earthly parents. He designs each one of us individually and in His perfect manner has a plan for our lives. He entrusts our earthly parents with our precious lives - birth, care, upbringing and primary education. If our parents have failed to do their duties, it is not because God does not love us. He has given each one of us the free will to fulfill or to neglect our roles and assignments. He will never violate our free will so long as we are on our journeys. He always watches over us, never abandoning us. Our hotline connection to Him is through prayer. Just because we cannot physically see

Him, does not mean He does not exist. I learned that clearly in Medjugorje. We are truly surrounded by the spiritual world even though we cannot see it with our human eyes. Here on earth, our physical bodies are merely the vehicles for our souls. In heaven, we will receive a glorified body which will not decay.[55] I will tell you how I learned this through a personal example that you might have experienced yourself.

My grandmother passed away (graduated) several years ago while living in my parents' house. The night before she died (graduated), I was joyfully talking to her. She seemed perfectly fine. Even though she exceeded 100 years of age, she was still fairly healthy and did not suffer from any significant physical ailments. The following morning, I found out she had unexpectedly passed (graduated) into eternal life as she slept. When I went to her room to see her, she was lying lifelessly on the bed. Usually people I loved either died (graduated) in a different country, different state, or while I was away. With my grandmother, the situation was different. As I watched her, I felt like shaking her to wake her up. She had been speaking to me several hours prior to that moment. What had changed about her? Her body was lying there and she looked almost the same. What if her skin seemed colorless and felt cold? What was suddenly missing in her that had previously filled her with vibrant life? Why couldn't she move? Clearly, she was not made only of a purely physical body but had a soul which was no longer there. It became clear to me how crucial the soul was to a physical body. The body eventually decomposes but the soul returns (graduates) back to its eternal home leaving behind everything material which constitutes a sense of security - the physical body, university degrees, professional titles,

---

[55] 1 Corinthians 15:39-44

large bank accounts, stock options, bonds, investments, fancy cars, large houses, prestigious employment and even our loved ones. Was there really any purpose behind my grandmother's whole life on earth? *Did you at all wonder why I kept on repeating the word "graduated" when I spoke about her death?* I believe that death is not the end to life but just the beginning of our post-graduation commencement. Death is the Graduation Day from our earthly education in the *School of Love*. I wished I had known this myself when my grandmother suddenly graduated. Although I would have still needed to process the resulting natural human grief from my loss, my initial attitude would have been much different.

Are you thinking *"what on earth is Samia saying? She just lost me completely!"* Do not worry. I have not suddenly lost my mind as we approach this book's conclusion of my journey thus far in life. It is quite the opposite. Life has never made more sense to me as it does today. Allow me to share with you another "Samia's theory" about what I think is the real purpose of our life journeys.

Similar to what I did when I went to study overseas in France for one year, each one of us is currently studying abroad in an intensive earthly educational program in the *School of Love*. To maximize this educational experience, we must always remember that our purpose here is to grow and mature spiritually through all the lessons we learn while living temporarily on earth. However, we must not forget that our permanent home is intended to be heaven. We must not forget that each one of us is entitled to deserve heaven only if we persevere in our pursuit of God. Heaven is a beautiful place filled with perfect love and harmony. Everything there is majestic and breathtaking. There is no hatred, no sickness, no jealousy, no violence, no grief or sadness, no pain and no selfishness. Heaven is just *perfect* and we cannot compare it to anything we have known here.

We are all one family,[56] regardless of our beliefs, ethnicity, color, nationality or gender and God is Our Heavenly Father.[57] He is a Spirit, **One** God existing through the mutual indwelling of **three** distinct, coeternal, coexistent and coequal **Persons**: Father, Son and Holy Spirit - the "Holy Trinity." God the Father and God the Holy Spirit have one nature, divine. God the Son, Jesus, is One Person with two distinct natures, human and divine. When He died on the cross, He died only in His human nature. Through His Divine Nature, He triumphed over death and resurrected on the third day. In our humanity, it is very hard for us to comprehend the concept of the Trinity, One God in Three Distinct Persons. Many students in the School do not understand God's triune nature. Worshipping a "triune" God does **not** imply polytheism or the worship of three separate gods. There is only **ONE** God who manifests Himself in **three distinct persons bound in perfect love, unity and cooperation**. This is a mystery that we will only fully come to understand after we graduate to our home in heaven. Meanwhile, we are required to practice the virtue of faith. While in prayer, the Lord gave me an earthly simile to the Trinity that I was able to comprehend with my finite human mind. He compared the Trinity to water. Water is a chemical compound essential in sustaining life in humans, plants, animals and every other living thing on earth. Although water exists in three distinct states - solid (ice or snow), liquid and gas (clouds or fog) – the essence remains the same, one and the same water. It can exist

---

[56] Ephesians 3:14-15, Ephesians 2:19
[57] Matthew 6:9

simultaneously in the three distinct states – for example a deep lake on a freezing foggy day. Due to the depth of the lake, the water on top is frozen (ice) while the water beneath the ice is liquid and the water in the air (fog) is gas. Likewise, God is three in one. God is the three Persons bound together by such a perfect love that they are One. St. John's statement that "God is love"[58] applies to all three persons simultaneously. The three Persons - One God - *is* Love. **Similar to water, God (the Holy Trinity) is essential in sustaining life in humans, plants and animals.**

When God the Son was incarnated taking on our human flesh and becoming the Son of Man, Jesus Christ, He was physically seen on earth in His "solid" state, *metaphorically speaking*, without leaving God the Father. He still retained His coequal, coeternal and coexistent essence with God the Father and God the Holy Spirit. Many students on earth have been brought up to believe that nobody knows, or should dare to say, who God is. They know Him intellectually as a concept or an idea of a power ruling the world. Therefore, they have been unable to comprehend how He could be in a "solid" tangible state, failing to recognize Him as their God. God the Son, Jesus Christ, appeared in His "solid" state, as the Son of Man. He still retained His divine nature and demonstrated it repeatedly through all the miracles He performed while on earth – healing the sick, healing of the blind, healing the paralytics, casting out demons and unclean spirits, forgiving the sins, raising the dead and finally His victorious resurrection from death on the third day. Nevertheless, many students' hearts are too blinded by Satan's poison, lies, evil and deceptive schemes that they cannot recognize their God in His human form even though all His divine works on earth spoke for Him.

---

[58] 1John 4:8

He was still able to appear to His apostles and to hundreds of other people[59] after His Resurrection. Jesus is the *"image of the invisible God, the firstborn of all creation."*[60] *"He delivered us from the power of darkness and transferred us to the kingdom of his beloved Son, in whom we have redemption and the forgiveness of sins.*[61] *For in Him were created all things in heaven and on earth, the visible and the invisible, whether thrones or dominions or principalities or powers; all things were created through Him and for Him. He is before all things, and in Him all things hold together. He is the head of the body, the church. He is the beginning, the firstborn from the dead, that in all things He Himself might be preeminent."*[62] Before His Passion, Jesus instructed His apostles: *"...I am the Way, the Truth and the Life. No one comes to the Father except through Me. If you know Me, then you will also know My Father. From now on you do know Him and have seen Him.... Do you not believe that I am in the Father and the Father is in Me? The words that I speak to you I do not speak on My own. The Father who dwells in Me is doing His works. Believe me that I am in the Father and the Father is in Me, or else, believe because of the works themselves."*[63] *"The Father and I are One."*[64]

After Jesus' resurrection, He ascended into heaven. He was lifted up on a cloud before the eyes of His apostles, leaving them with the promise to send the Holy Spirit. The Holy Spirit is the third Person of the Trinity, a

---

[59] Matthew 28: 1-20, Mark 16: 1-20, Luke 24: 1-53, John 20:1-30, 21:1-25, Acts 1:1-12

[60] Colossians 1:15

[61] Colossians 1:13-14

[62] Colossians 1: 16-18

[63] John 14: 6-8, 10-11

[64] John 10:30

manifestation of our Father's continuous LOVE. Jesus told His apostles: *"And I will ask the Father, and He will give you another Advocate to be with you always, the Spirit of Truth, which the world cannot accept, because it neither sees nor knows it. But you know it, because it remains with you, and will be in you. I will not leave you orphans; I will come to you."*[65]

We are *all* His Precious Children.[66] He has knit us carefully in the womb[67] and has even named each one of us while in our earthly mother's womb;[68]we are all brothers and sisters. Our Father has decided to send us abroad to study temporarily on earth. The nationality there is called Humanity. The languages we speak vary, depending on our role and assignment throughout our education. We are all enrolled in the same school called *School of Love.* Earth is much different than our home in heaven. We need to wear a special costume specifically designed to host our souls while in this foreign, earthly environment. This costume is called a "physical body" and is made of an interesting material called "flesh." Our humanity is created in the divine image and likeness of the Holy Trinity.[69] Each detail of our costumes is designed precisely, depending on the special role we play or the assignment each of us is given in the *School of Love.* The school operates similarly to a theatrical play of life and we are assigned different roles in this play. There are many different characters involved. The characters wear a variety of costumes with different colors and designs, depending on the various roles in the play. The diversity of costumes is crucial as it keeps the

---

[65] John 14:16-18
[66] 1 John 3:1
[67] Psalm 139:13
[68] Isaiah 49:1
[69] Genesis 1: 26-27

play inspiring and challenging to everyone involved. If all the costumes were alike, the play would be too boring and uninteresting. Some key characters have long serious roles and last throughout the play. Others have very small roles and leave the play soon after their part is over. Some characters have to die tragically while others die from illnesses or natural causes. Each role is perfectly written by the screenwriter, our Heavenly Father. He writes each role and each script perfectly but He gives the characters the liberty to improvise during the play cautioning against the dangers of departing completely from the script.

While in the *School of Love*, our Father gives each one of us a unique student identification card called "fingerprint" hoping that these fingerprints will remind us of how special we are. Nobody else alive now – or in the past or in the future - has the same fingerprint. He tells us that even the very hairs on our heads are all numbered![70] He knows that due to our studying abroad, the earthly temptations will be very influential and seductive, causing us to forget about Him, about each other, about our permanent home in heaven, and about our true identities of who we truly are: the children of God.

We have been sent to this intensive school to advance our education in a very important topic, the course of LOVE. Our Father knows that the more we advance in the course of LOVE, the larger our capacity will be to experience and enjoy His love for us. In heaven, love naturally fills everyone and everything. Our Father, who is LOVE,[71] has created everything with love in harmony with His essence. There is no challenge to love others in heaven.

---

[70] Matthew 10:30
[71] 1 John: 4:8

It is the natural state of every spirit there. All the siblings love each other without any self-interest, jealousy or comparisons.

To truly master LOVE, we are required to take some very difficult classes which are crucial in accelerating our learning process. Such classes include: suffering, sacrifice, self-giving, pain and sickness. When these classes become too hard, He "gifts" us with tears to diffuse the pressure. He cautions us that with each of these classes, there might be an additional laboratory course, called "evil." This course is manipulated by a very deceptive and bitter con-artist called Satan. He has been very enraged with our Father, the school's Principal, as he is very jealous of all of us, the students, because the Principal loves each one of us. Satan wants to do everything possible within his power to make us fail[72] all the classes and become bitter with our Heavenly Father who has sent us here to study. Satan's hope is to greatly influence us with his own laboratory course so that we would eventually reject our Father here on earth and even after our graduation. His number-one strategy is to attempt to inject our minds with his toxic venoms of **fear, mistrust and doubt**. Fear is usually an indication of lack of faith and trust in our Father's LOVE for us. Faith and trust are essential virtues and ingredients to sustain us in our growth while abroad. Our Heavenly Father tells us that the only way Satan could claim us, is if we give up on our Father's LOVE for us. Our Father reminds us that His love will always be greater than any disobedience or offense against Him. **He will always forgive us, no matter what, if we ask Him for forgiveness with repentant and humble hearts.** We just need to be aware of Satan's misleading ways and not fall for his deceptive schemes. Satan's laboratory

---

[72] Revelations 12:17

course is an additional challenge in all our courses. The better we deal with the devil's trials and persecutions, the greater we grow in faith, trust, hope and especially LOVE. It is precisely through these "tensions" that LOVE growth is accelerated. That is why we do not grow the same way in heaven as everything is perfectly harmonious there. These tensions do not exist there hence, there are no challenges. Our Father promises to dismiss Satan and his followers to his own hellfire once we all had graduated.[73] After that, Our Father will have no purpose for him. He tells us that when these courses get painfully difficult, we should remember that there is always a lesson to be learned in each course. We need to remind ourselves to ask the question: *What am I supposed to learn from this?* This question will help us to see these classes in a more positive light and therefore to accept the challenge to grow with LOVE.

Because our Heavenly Father loves us, He also includes supportive classes and graces such as forgiveness, trust, faith, hope, mercy, joy, patience, perseverance, compassion, understanding and peace. He emphasizes that the forgiveness course is very important. We need to continuously practice it as it is essential to our growth in LOVE. He adds that we must always forgive others but also forgive ourselves. If we have difficulties with this course, He offers to give us assistance with all the graces that we need including one of "laughter" to compensate for the difficult times during these courses.

As the Principal of the *School of Love*, Our Father has the final authority over all matters related to our educational experience but he does not want to be a dictatorial type. He tells us that we will be given much free liberty

---

[73] Matthew 25:41

through something called "free will" as we practice our roles and completed our assignments. Some roles are easier than others. Some will be more challenging due to the persecutions and the adversities that will be faced. The difficult roles are accompanied by greater opportunities to love. Our Father also gives each of us a "special assignment." This assignment can only be performed by each specific person. Even though it might appear that some assignments are more important than others, He assures us that they are all equally important in His eyes. We each need to complete our assignment before graduation. Once the assignment is completed, we can graduate and return home. To help with our assignment, He forms us in different groups to assist one another. Each group is called a "family." Our family is the primary place we learn about and practice LOVE. It is the place where the challenges to love and to forgive are the greatest because of our fallen human nature and woundedness which creates tensions with frequent contact. However, this group would also be a great source of support and love. He gives each one of us a "father" and a "mother" who are the primary two persons to initially teach us about LOVE. Parents represent and reflect God and His love for us. If we are raised in a loving family with loving parents, our perception of God and His love for us is mirrored in a positive and healthy way. Unfortunately, Satan knows this and consequently, he launches attacks on the family to cause problems or even permanent division called "divorce." Unfortunately, divorces cause many wounds in the hearts and souls of children as it shakes their foundations and their bonding with each parent. Divorce affects their self-esteem, their sense of belonging, their security in life but most importantly their trust in their parents which consequently results in their mistrust in God. How can a child trust the "invisible" Heavenly Father, if the child cannot even trust the visible earthly father or mother? This wound usually causes a severe breach in the relationship of the child with God. Satan loves to inject his lies into these wounds to cause much shame and fear by making the child feel unworthy, unlovable, guilty, responsible and abandoned. To protect the family unit, our Father asks families to pray together daily to obtain spiritual protection and graces. Just as the family unit does everything possible to guard against physical harm, it also needs to do everything possible to protect itself from spiritual threats. Family prayer is the answer to obtain heavenly assistance and protection.

Our Father reminds us that His love for us is very maternal. *"Can a mother forget her infant, be without tenderness for the child of her womb? Even should she forget, I will never forget you. See, upon the palm of my hands I have written your name."*[74] He will always be watching over us. We can always call Him for help.[75] Our earthly phones may not be used for this; we need to use the spiritual phone for the perfect connection. He gives us a powerful mobile phone called *Prayer* which can help us to obtain anything that we ask,[76] if it is good for our growth and education. To make this call, we must turn inwardly to our hearts. He tells us that He will always be available through prayer, twenty-four hours a day. His line is never busy. He promises to never place us on hold and to always pick up our calls.[77] He cautions us that to have a good telephone connection with Him, we must be focused and in silence to be able to connect inwardly.[78] Although our Father

---

[74] Isaiah 49:15-16
[75] Psalm 50:15
[76] Mark 11:24
[77] Isaiah 58:9
[78] Matthew 6:6

already knows all our needs before we ask Him,[79] He wants us to pray and connect with Him. Prayer is a very powerful instrument for us. We need to pray for each other as this is one of the ways we express our love for another and increase our own capacity to love.[80] Prayer strengthens us during temptations and trials as the flesh is weak even though the spirit is willing.[81] Prayer helps us as we fight against pride to strive for humility. When we pray, we acknowledge our weaknesses and limitations as humans; we humble ourselves before God's might.[82] *"...for everyone who exalts himself will be humbled and the one who humbles himself will be exalted."*[83]

Jesus the Lord and God was incarnated to testify to the truth and He asks us to seek His ways by always seeking "truth." He tells us: "...*everyone who belongs to the truth listens to my voice.*"[84] He cautions us that during our years abroad, we will be offered many false truths by His enemy, Satan, whose only objective is to destroy our educational experience and to teach us additional non-recommended classes on judgment, pride, hatred, division, destruction, denial, selfishness and self-righteousness. Our Lord commands us to stop judging others or we will be judged the same way ourselves with the same measure we apply to others. He reminds us to first see our own errors and imperfections before pointing out those of another.[85]

Our Father has created our human souls and spirits to always thirst for Him as He is the fountain of wisdom and source of eternal love. He teaches

---

[79] Matthew 6:8
[80] James 5:16
[81] Mark 14:38
[82] 1Peter 5:6
[83] Luke 18:14
[84] John 18:37
[85] Matthew 7:1-5

us through, Saint Augustine – a faithful student who has graduated in the year 430 – to seek truth and to find God, like Augustine did, eventually becoming a saint. Augustine had been living under Satan's spell for many years and was hell-bent on the wrong path. He is remembered for his famous sentence in his autobiographical book:[86] *"You made us for Yourself, and our heart is restless until it finds it place of rest in You."* St. Augustine sought truth and found God in whom his restless heart was able to find peace. As a result, inflamed with the Lord Jesus' love, he devoted his life to teach about God and the faith.

To keep us on track, Our Father reminds us to always read His "love letter" - the *Holy Bible* as it will teach us more about Him and the School's history and objective. Even though His letter might seem long or too historical, He assures us that when we need answers to our questions while on the journey, He will often speak through it to our hearts. The letter is composed of two important parts that are called the "Old Testament" and the "New Testament." The Old Testament reminds us of the beginning of the *School of Love*. It narrates how our Heavenly Father formed everything around the school to enhance our education. He created everything that is familiar to us now, time and space – earth, water, sky, vegetation and animals.[87] After Our Father created our school's environment, He created our first spiritual brother and sister, Adam and Eve. He then looked at everything that He had made and He found it very good.[88] Into this goodness of our Father's creation, Satan insinuated his evil head. Unfortunately, Adam and

---

[86] Augustine. *The Confessions of Saint Augustine.* Baker Book House, 2005, 17.
[87] Genesis 1: 1-25
[88] Genesis 1:31

Eve fell into the snares of Satan because they did not keep God's saving commandments not to eat from the fruit of the Tree of Knowledge of Good and Evil. Their fall affected all humanity. As a result, even though Adam and Eve graduated, they could not go back to their eternal home because they had gravely disobeyed our Father. Thus, it is believed that Adam and Eve – along with other faithful graduating souls who followed, stayed in an exiled place for thousands of years. Our Father's love letter promised us salvation throughout the history in the Old Testament that He would redeem us from the snares of Satan by coming to earth Himself as the Messiah, the Anointed One, known to us as God's only Son, Jesus Christ.

As we are taught in the New Testament, God reopened the gates of heaven to all His children through the most important historical events in the School's history: the Passion, Death on the cross and Resurrection from death of His only Son, our Lord Jesus Christ. Our Father, out of **His perfect love for all of us,** sent us His Son. Jesus humbled Himself completely, coming down to earth and becoming one of us through His own incarnation, taking on our earthly nature, as prophesized in the Old Testament: "... *the virgin shall be with child, and bear a son, and shall name him Immanuel,*"[89] a *"name which means 'God is with us.'"*[90] Jesus' birth in Bethlehem,[91] His ministry,[92] His passion and death[93] and His resurrection[94] were prophesized in the Old Testament. Tragically, motivated by pride, ignorance, jealousy and fear, Jesus' own betrayed Him and condemned Him to death by crucifixion.

---

[89] Isaiah 7:14, see also Matthew 1:23
[90] Mathew 1:23
[91] Micah 5:2
[92] Isaiah 61:1-2, Luke 4:16-21
[93] Isaiah 53:7-11
[94] Hosea 6:2

Despite this, Jesus taught us the biggest lesson in LOVE and forgiveness as He said, while dying on the cross *"Father, forgive them, they know not what they do."*[95] Jesus also taught us during His final twenty-four hours that LOVE is not a **feeling**. LOVE is a **decision**. He was in such great agony as He prayed in the Garden of Gethsemane. He prayed so fervently that his sweat became drops of blood falling on the ground.[96] Despite His great agony and the darkness in His soul, He decided to drink the cup of suffering and thus demonstrated His great LOVE for all of us as He did the will of God the Father. While on the cross, He gave us His very own Mother Mary as our mother, delegating His apostle John as her son.[97] Our Heavenly Father chose Mary from amongst all women because of her incredible humility, love and total surrender to His divine will. Even though she was a virgin when the angel announced to Mary that she would conceive the Son of God through the overshadowing of the Holy Spirit,[98]she understood all the ridicule and persecutions she would have to face as a result of her out-of-wedlock pregnancy. Mary was only betrothed (engaged) to Joseph and they were not living together. In the strict culture of that day - which is very similar to the one in which I was raised - she could have been stoned to death but Mary gave her total surrender and said YES to God when she replied with much humility and love: *"…Behold, I am the handmaid of the Lord. Be it done unto me according to your word."*[99] Our Lord Jesus and Mary model to us

---

[95] Luke 23:34
[96] Luke 22:44
[97] John 19: 26-27
[98] Luke 1:35
[99] Luke 1:38

the kind of life we should lead in this school – a life of forgiveness, humility, faith, simplicity and total surrender to God's divine will.

Graduation is the only guaranteed event after conception that everyone will experience on earth. As part of our graduation, we will need to leave our physical body on earth. We will no longer need the earthly bodies when we return home to heaven as they are not needed there. Instead, we will receive later glorified bodies.[100] Most of us might get so attached to our earthly journeys that we might eventually forget that we are temporarily studying on earth. Upon graduation some of us might still be so influenced by Satan's classes and schemes that we would reject God despite all His love for us. We might still be filled with much hatred and rage against Him. In this event, even though He does not wish this for any of His beloved children, He will need to send us to another permanent home besides heaven, called hell. Since everything in heaven is in a state of perfect love, harmony and peace, hell is a place where there is no love, no harmony and no peace. It is a requirement in heaven to be filled with love and to discard any negativity we might have picked up while studying on earth. If we pick up any earthly toxins that pollute our spirits, such as lack of love, hatred, unforgiveness and judgment of others, we will need to go to a place annexed to heaven called purgatory to purge ourselves of all the harmful effects of these toxins.[101] This place is similar to a "steam room." We will welcome the positive benefits it will produce in our spirits and eventually enable us to be with our Father who is perfect LOVE. Whether we go directly to heaven or to purgatory, we will

---

[100] 1Corinthians 15:39-44
[101] 2Maccabees 12:42-46, Luke 12:58-59, Revelations 21:27, 1Corinthians 3:10-15

always remain in communion – that is spiritual union - with our remaining loved ones and siblings who are still studying on earth.

We need to practice LOVE in everything we do, especially with our families, with each other, with strangers and even with our enemies. Our Lord asks us to do everything with LOVE. He commanded us: "*...love one another as I love you. No one has greater love than this, to lay down one's life for one's friends.*"[102] Our Lord's beloved apostle John also states: "*Whoever is without love does not know God; for God is Love.*"[103] Things have no value if they are not done with LOVE. LOVE should be the ultimate objective of everything we do and the reason we would do it. In fact, I believe that once we graduate and return to our Lord in heaven, He will ask us only one question: **How much did you LOVE?**

Mother Teresa of Calcutta graduated in 1997 and exemplified how to practice LOVE in everything and with everyone. For most of her life, she ministered to the poorest of the poor, the sick, the orphaned and the dying. In her great love, she served everyone equally without any discrimination, regardless of religion, creed, color or nationality. She saw everyone as a precious child of God. She frequently stated during her interviews: "*It is not how much we do, but how much love we put in the doing. It is not how much we give, but how much love we put in the giving. We can do no great things, only small things with great love. If we really want to LOVE, we must learn how to FORGIVE. There is a terrible hunger for love. We all experience that in our lives – the pain, the loneliness. We must have the courage to recognize*

---

[102] John 15:12-14
[103] 1John 4:8

it. The poor you may have right in your own family. Find them. Love them."[104]

After having shared my life's journey with you, you might be wondering why our Heavenly Father has allowed me to have miraculous experiences on my journey since many people do not. You might be judging your life and discounting it as less important than mine in comparison. Believe me when I say, God does *not* love me or anyone else anymore than He loves YOU. He loves us all equally as His Children. He does not have preferential treatment between us.[105] He has given each one of us a different assignment and role which are equally important to Him. The mother who is working at home raising her children has an assignment *as* important as the assignment of any corporate executive. I dare to say she has more critical responsibilities. God has entrusted her with the lives of one or more of His precious children. Nothing is more important to God than our lives. I have never had the great privilege of bearing a child myself and only God knows if this is still part of my assignment, after I meet and marry my soulmate. I greatly admire any woman or man who is raising a family! I believe this is one of the most important assignments anyone can ever have. May our Heavenly Father richly bless your hearts and families and give you all the graces that you need to persevere through this assignment!

While on earth, I believe part of my assignment is to guide my siblings back to our Father's loving heart and to be one of the many messengers of His love. I truly believe that this *is* the reason for this book. *Without God, my*

---

[104] *Mother Teresa (1986).* DVD Film by Ann Jeanette Petrie with a narration by Richard Attenborough. www.motherteresa.film.com
[105] Acts: 10: 34-35; Luke 20:21

life has no meaning. I will always connect with Him through prayer. As I persevere in my human education and journey, I think of myself as a pencil with which Our Heavenly Father writes my assignment for His Glory. Every time I break, He sharpens me slowly and gently. He will keep on sharpening me until I complete my assignment and am back in His loving arms. This day will be a glorious one for me as it will be my final Graduation Day. I anticipate that majestic graduation party which our Heavenly Father will hold in my honor after I graduate from this *School of Love* on earth and return to our eternal home, heaven.

Now I pray that you will open your heart to receive His love as He speaks to you!

Chapter Seventeen

MESSAGE OF LOVE

"This is my commandment: love one another as I love you. No one has greater love than this, to lay down one's life for one's friends. You are my friends if you do what I command you."

\- John 15:12-15

T his chapter is intended to be read after you have completed reading the previous chapters. I hope that you are not skipping through this book and just jumping to the end. If you are, I kindly ask you to go back and read all the chapters preceding this one, particularly Chapter Thirteen. Otherwise, this chapter will not make sense to you and you might severely misjudge me and thus waste the Lord's intended message for **YOU**.

Throughout the year 2006-2007, the Lord spoke to my heart often to instruct me, to console me through my hardships and to guide me on various aspects of my life's journey. Initially, I was not planning on including any of the words He spoke as they were personal and related directly to the events occurring in my life. He gave me these words over the course of thirteen months. After much prayer, the Lord instructed me to include them in my book. While these words were initially spoken for *my* journey's benefit, the Lord told me that He will be now speaking directly to **YOU** through them for your **OWN** journey's benefit. He specifically requested that I share them with **you**. This will be a very intimate conversation between **you** and the Lord. These words are no longer for me but will become an additional educational course to **your** earthly education in your School of Love, just like they are now part of mine. These words will have a different meaning to **you** than they did to me. I pray that you will give yourself permission to experience His love as you read these words. The words of love are specifically for **you**. He wants you to experience His love. He will not force you. He will only knock on the door of your heart to speak with you and will always love you regardless of your response!

Let me remind you that I am only the Lord's humble messenger with the assignment to convey His love to you. Since I am your spiritual sister, this is part of my life's journey, one of my *School of Love's* assignments. The content of the words below does not elevate me above you or anyone else. We are all equal as His beloved Children. The words that follow give each of us loving directions to guide and help us as we journey here on earth while away from our real home, heaven. As the Lord taught me: *"Truth never needs to be proven. It stands on its own."*

I pray for your protection as I cover you completely with the Precious Blood of Jesus. I pray that your guardian angel shields and protects you and your loved ones. I bind in the name of Jesus Christ any demonic spirits around you: *You demonic spirits have NO authority to interfere with the message that Jesus has for my brother or sister. Leave immediately without harming or disturbing anyone and allow the Lord Jesus to deal with you as He sees fit.*

The following paragraphs in this chapter are the words that over a period of thirteen months, I heard the Lord Jesus speak to my heart while in deep prayer.[106] Receive *Jesus'* peace and love as *He* speaks to your heart now.

"My Sweet Child,

"I have been asking you to give Me thirty days of your life. You have allowed many things to come between us, between you and your book. I am not rebuking you. I am only speaking words of truth to your heart. You get easily frustrated and often are filled with despair. I tell you that I need your cooperation for what is next. Your soul, and not just your body, needs to be ready. Train your soul as hard as you train your body when you exercise. Just as you feel your body's muscles growing, you need to experience that also with your soul.

"Overcome your temptations. I need for you to remain united to Me. Every time you commit sins, you cut off our union. You need to say "no" to sin to become stronger with the graces I am giving you. Resist temptations and you will become stronger. That is how you train your will. You practice until it becomes second nature to you. I love you, My sweet child. I am not

---

[106] This is considered a private revelation. There are two kinds of revelations: 1) universal public revelations, which are contained in the Bible or in the deposit of Apostolic tradition transmitted by the Church; these public revelations ended with the preaching of the Apostles and must be believed by all; (2) private revelations which are constantly occurring among Christians. When the Church approves private revelations, she declares only that there is nothing in them contrary to faith or good morals, and that they may be read without danger or even with profit; no obligation is thereby imposed on the faithful to believe them. This particular private revelation has not been officially approved by or disapproved by the Church.

rebuking you but loving you most tenderly. I want you to be trained for what is ahead of us so that I can manifest through you most powerfully. Everything you have had glimpses of will come to fulfillment in due time. You have received confirmations from so many of My children, including your friend.[107] Your life is anointed and you have been chosen to bring peace. Your book will be completed and I will inspire it completely. My Spirit will speak through it. Do not pressure yourself. You just need to remain a clean vessel. Always remain humble, loving, gentle and meek. Pray, My sweet child. I will give you the words. Remain united to My Sacred Heart and to the heart of My beloved Mother who has chosen you. Remain close to her heart. Hold on to your rosary and meditate on it. Let your fingers become so accustomed to praying it that they will feel abandoned without it.

" I want your full attention. Do it for My Glory. Do it for the Glory of the Holy Trinity. Do not let anything distract you. Remain focused. Allow Me to work through you. All will come to pass. The words that I have spoken to you will be fulfilled. Do not worry about your next employment. Do not occupy yourself with that for now. I promised to bring it to you. I want you to do nothing except work on your book. That needs to be your priority. Please heed My words, My precious child. I need you to understand the urgency of what I am telling you.

"Always be disciplined. Remember the discipline with which I lived. I made time for prayer, time to be alone with My Heavenly Father away from My disciples. I ask you to do the same with your life. I want to have your full attention and focus. The struggle cannot be won without strict discipline. Designate specific hours of your day to be with Me in adoration. Do not

---

[107]In this specific situation, the Lord is referring to my friend Monica.

bring your mobile phone or anything else that might distract you. I will remind you of memories and will inspire the words for your book that My other children can connect to them. Write, My child. I will give you all the words of love. Do not be anxious. The Spirit will inspire you with the words.

"Do not worry about your finances. I will provide you with everything that you will need daily. Meditate often on My Words in the Gospel of Matthew 6:24-34.[108] These are My words and promise to you.

"I am trying to teach you slowly how to overcome the weaknesses of your flesh. The flesh is demanding but it cannot overpower the soul. You have to strictly train your soul to control all the desires of the flesh. I know how painful that is. I spent forty days in the desert with very painful temptations. Dedicate hours of your day to be with Me and stick to them.

"Physical exercise is very important to release your tensions and relax your mind. It will help you refocus and get grounded again mentally and physically.

---

[108] "No one can serve two masters. He will either hate one and love the other, or be devoted to one and despise the other. You cannot serve God and mammon. Therefore I tell you, do not worry about your life, what you will eat [or drink], or about your body, what you will wear. Is not life more than food and the body more than clothing? Look at the birds in the sky; they do not sow or reap, they gather nothing into barns, yet your heavenly Father feeds them. Are not you more important than they? Can any of you by worrying add a single moment to your life-span? Why are you anxious about clothes? Learn from the way the wild flowers grow. They do not work or spin. But I tell you that not even Solomon in all his splendor was clothed like one of them. If God so clothes the grass of the field, which grows today and is thrown into the oven tomorrow, will he not much more provide for you, O you of little faith? So do not worry and say, 'What are we to eat?' or 'What are we to drink?' or 'What are we to wear?' All these things the pagans seek. Your heavenly Father knows that you need them all. But seek first the kingdom [of God] and his righteousness, and all these things will be given you besides. Do not worry about tomorrow; tomorrow will take care of itself. Sufficient for a day is its own evil. "

"Be at peace with everyone around you, especially your family. You need your family's support and strength. Be compassionate and loving with your parents. I am healing your relationship with them. You need to be at peace with them to be able to carry the mission ahead of you. Always take refuge in My Heart. I want you to be at peace.

"Remember My Passion. Meditate on My Passion and how I reacted to My trials and the false accusations. I always reacted with peace, love and obedience. Never entertain the plots of the enemy in your life. Division and friction always come from him.

"Truth never needs to be proven. It stands on its own. Remember that always. When you know the truth in your heart, you will remain peaceful, no matter what is coming against you. Of course you will be attacked in the world. You are not greater than your Master. Welcome the attacks with love, joy, peace and humility. I will use everything you offer up to Me to save many souls.

"Your will was often broken when you were a child. You were taught to say "no" or "yes" when it was not your true will. Now you are learning to stand for the truth but you must do everything with love and humility.

Keep your heart clean, slow to anger, gentle and meek. Clothe yourself with My love and humility. Open your mouth only to defend others or say words of praise about them. Otherwise, keep a guard on your tongue and on what comes out of your mouth.

"What will it take for you to trust in My love for you? Do not seek the world's love or praise. It will always disappoint you. Seek first My Kingdom; everything else will be given to you. We are all united together with you in heaven. Stay connected to Me and I will guide you step by step. Remember to

close your eyes, take a deep breath and consult with Me about everything. Seek My will in everything. I am fine-tuning you. You have great healings ahead of you.

"Things are not always as they appear in life. It was in the midst of darkness that I triumphed over sin victoriously. No prayer you have made for anyone has gone unheard or unanswered.

"I heard your supplications and outcries, I heard the outcry of your heart. None have fallen on deaf ears. You are the jewel of My Eye. I love you! Your heart aches to hear those words, I know. Trust Me for I am your Jesus. I have wiped your tears often. Do not despair. Receive graces from My Victory over Satan. The enemy rejoices in destroying your plans and working against you. Always ask others for prayers but entrust your deepest thoughts to Me. Persevere and do not give up. It might look like you have lost the struggle, but you have not. I am strengthening you. I know how much you have endured in life. I know how much you have suffered. Believe Me when I tell you that nothing has been in vain in your life.

"You are having a very hard time understanding My Will. You are questioning everything including what I am saying to you right now. Do not doubt My Voice. You know the Voice of Truth. Do not think I have abandoned you, not even for a second. You and I are more united than ever. I have been purifying your soul, making it fertile, ready for what is ahead. You need this time of preparation. Do not take lightly what is in store for the world. You have an important mission ahead. You need to remain focused and united to My heart. Do not fear. Do not worry.

"Your life is not a failure. Stop judging it from the world's eyes. My sweet child, I am trying to teach you to unite to Me in everything. Do not

seek the world's consolation or love. It will always disappoint you, like it did Me. Humanity is weak and self-seeking. True love is very rare on earth. You know that already. Unite your heart completely to Mine. Take refuge in My Heart. I have not and will never abandon you. Your trials have been lengthy and may seem meaningless to you but trust in My mercy and love. Come and immerse yourself in My Heart.

"Why do you hold on precisely when I ask you to let go, and let go completely? You are standing in the way and delaying the healing process. You often misread and misinterpret things. Conflict comes from the devil, not Me. Conflict is not an instrument of God but the enemy. I will bring goodness from any situation. I bring healing. Rejoice in your suffering as I am using it for the atonement of specific sins. Know that I also love everyone. Know that I died for everyone. People are wounded. Despite the appearance of luxury, they feel emptier than ever. Do not crucify yourself when it is not needed. Trust your heart. People who have hurt you projected their wounds and feelings of guilt and resentment upon you. People love you with their capacity to love. Do not dismiss what you do in their lives. You would be doing them a tremendous injustice. You bring them tremendous healings through your prayers, fasting, Masses and mostly suffering. I will not let that go unrewarded.

"Keep your heart open and clean. I want you to give Me all the resentment and hurt that you are turning inward. The enemy wants to use that to torture and destroy you. Surrender everything to Me right now and do not be afraid. I will NEVER fail you. You are My faithful and obedient servant.

"Stop judging others. I want you to be completely peaceful, filled with Me. Nothing in your life has ever been too late. Every day is a new beginning and new start. Remember that I make everything new. I will renew you but I need your participation. I need your help and obedience. Please make yourself a priority for now. Work on yourself. Place yourself first. I am not asking you to be selfish, I just need your undivided attention for now to take away the bitterness and anxiety you are feeling. I am purifying and sanctifying your heart and soul, day by day, minute by minute.

"Fasting is so crucial for your growth. You have to be able to tame your flesh in order to strengthen your soul. When you feel tempted to eat, say a Chaplet of Divine Mercy[109] every time. I promise to take the temptation away from you. Pray so that you will not be tempted.

"Prayer is your answer to everything in life. It connects you to the Heart of the Father and Mine. We will strengthen you and defend you. That is why you have to always stay in prayer. You are asking Me what that means. It means to connect to Me in everything. The less you are "stuffed" with worldly things, the clearer is your perception and hearing. The more "stuffed" you are with food or other people, the less time you have to hear My Voice. You would be too distracted and focused elsewhere. Focus on Me. Love Me. Talk to Me. Cry to Me. Vent to Me. Eat My Spiritual Food. Listen to My Voice and Advice. I promise to give you everything you need. You will have your joy back when you experience My Love in fullness.

---

[109] To obtain further information on the Chaplet of Divine Mercy, please visit: www.ewtn.com/devotionals/mercy/mmap.htm

"Heaven is praying for you. You are not alone and will never be alone. Your life is about to change dramatically. I want you to be ready. Unite yourself completely to Me. Do not ever doubt how special you are to My Mother. She has been interceding for you. Do not depart from her. Do not doubt. Do not fear. Do not be afraid to receive My love for you. This is not about you or for your own glory. Do not be afraid to accept it. As long as you are united to My Heart, I will not allow you to drift away. We are one, My child. I will work through you and within you. What is ahead will not be easy but I have already conquered death; so nothing is impossible. I ask you to take things seriously. Do not worry about your finances. I am with you providing for your daily needs.

"So many things will be done through your journey, through your person. You see now why you have been so attacked all your life. Remain humble and meek always. Remain peaceful and loving. Do not judge. Some will be jealous of the gifts which I have given to you. Do not hold that against them. It takes and requires great love to truly love others without self-interest. That is something you will experience in heaven all the time. There will be no need for comparison there. Everyone sees themselves in relationship to the Father, in union with Me, the Son.

"There are no blind alleys when you seek Me, you can never use up My grace, there will always be more. Faith is the extent of your beliefs. Do not place limits on Me, the Limitless One. I love you My child!"

About the Author

Samia Mary Zumout (pronounced "Samya") was born in Jordan in the Middle East to a Catholic family. Her family immigrated to the United States in 1983 when she was thirteen years old. Samia attended the University of California at Davis where she received Bachelor of Arts degrees in International Relations and also French. She later received her Juris Doctorate from the University of San Francisco School of Law. Samia is fluent in four languages: English, Arabic, Spanish and French.

In 1990 after Samia studied in France for one year, she went backpacking throughout Europe with a couple of friends. During the trip, Samia traveled to Medjugorje in the country of Bosnia-Herzegovina (formerly known as Yugoslavia) where our Blessed Mother Mary has been allegedly appearing daily since 1981. This experience changed Samia's life as she experienced in her heart, for the first time in her life, our Lord Jesus' immense love for her in a very profound and life-changing way. Our Blessed Mother Mary led her on her path to living a sacramental life centered on the Eucharist. Samia has consecrated her life to serve our Lord Jesus Christ. This was also the beginning of Samia's own inner-healing journey and prayer ministry that led her to become a messenger and an instrument of God's healing love to His children.

Professionally, Samia worked as a lawyer for over ten years. However, in her personal life, she spent extensive time in the inner-healing and evangelization ministries over the past eight years. She aggressively pursued her own inner-healing which allowed her later to minister to others on their own healing journeys - especially after having been thoroughly trained in both basic and advanced courses in Francis McNutt's Christian School of Healing Prayer and also *Theophostic Prayer Ministry* as well as other healing prayer ministries

In June 2006, Samia felt a strong desire in her heart to write her first autobiographical book, *The Bridge between the East and West: A Journey to Truth through His Love.* While in deep prayer, the Lord Jesus confirmed to Samia that writing this book was an important part of her life's mission as it would bring the Lord closer to the hearts of many who would experience His healing love while reading about her life's journey. The Lord Jesus instructed Samia that it would only take her 30 days to write the book if she lived a sacramental life centered on the Eucharist, deep prayer and fasting throughout that period. Samia began writing the book on July 17, 2007 and the book was completed on August 15, 2007, exactly 30 days later.

In July 2008, Samia was invited to Twin Falls, Idaho, to do missionary work at St. Edward's Catholic Parish until May 2009. Samia set aside her career as an attorney to follow God's Will in her life by serving Him on a full-time basis to bring His healing love and presence to His hurting children.

In June 2009, Samia returned to Sacramento, California to continue her ministry through the generosity of Immaculate Conception Parish in Sacramento, our Lord Jesus has provided her with an office space to provide for her inner-healing prayer ministry. In addition, Samia travels nationally and internationally to give her testimony and speak on various topics related to the Catholic faith and inner-healing.

Contact Information

If you have any comments or feedback about the book, or if you would like to invite the author to speak at your Church or to your group, please contact the author at:

Samia Zumout

P.O. Box: 189451

Sacramento, CA 95818

E-mail: samiazumout@yahoo.com

www.samiazumout.com

www.bridgebetweeneastandwest.com

You can order more copies of the book at:

http://booklocker.com/books/3893.html
or
www.samiazumout.com

LaVergne, TN USA
26 February 2011
218043LV00002B/2/P